TRAINING WITHIN INDUSTRY MATERIALS

Bulletin Series

T0383151

TRAINING WITHIN INDUSTRY MATERIALS

Bulletin Series

Bulletins Issued by Training Within Industry and Outlines of the Training Within Industry Programs for War Plants and Essential Services

WAR MANPOWER COMMISSION

Bureau of Training

Training Within Industry Service

September 1945

Originally published as *The Training Within Industry Program Bulletin Series*, released individually between 1940-45 by the War Manpower Commission of the Bureau of Training, Washington, District of Columbia.

Enna Products
1602 Carolina St.
Suite B3
Bellingham, WA 98229
Telephone: (360) 306-5369
Fax: (905) 481-0756
E-mail: info@enna.com

Cover design/illustrations by Khemanand Shiwram
Editing/typography by Tracy S. Epley

Library of Congress Cataloging-in-Publication Data

United States. Bureau of Training. War Manpower Commission. 1940-45
    The Training Within Industry Program Bulletin Series.

    Includes Index
    ISBN 978-1-897363-91-1

    1. Training Within Industry 2. Training of employees 3. Organizational change
4. Productivity–Increasing through training   I. Title

Dedicated to the men and women of The Greatest Generation.

I—Training Within Industry Bulletins

Training Within Industry was organized in August 1940. Its immediate purpose, as far as could be seen then, was to provide a clearing–house service in industrial training techniques, and to make training consultation available to contractors which requested this service. This objective, of course, expanded as conditions of war production changed.

During the first year of existence a number of bulletins on the need for training in expanding plants and on generally accepted training techniques were written for defense contractors. Later a few bulletins were added to the series— in order to provide materials needed in the T. W. I. programs.

This section includes, in their latest editions, all of the Training Within Industry bulletins. Many of them, since they were prepared for use on problems of conversion and expansion, were allowed to go out of print when war production struck its full stride and so have not been distributed during the past two to three years. They are included in this complete set in order to give a picture of industrial conditions and problems at the time they were written.

TABLE OF CONTENTS

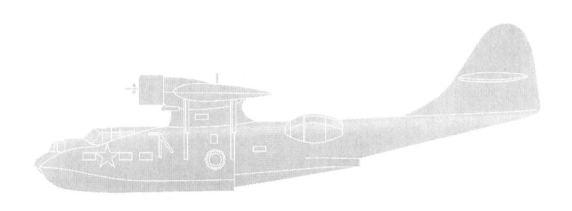

TRAINING   WITHIN   INDUSTRY

THE TWI JOB   THE COMPANY JOB

GET TOP MANAGEMENT TO ACCEPT THE RESPONSIBILITY →

← **ESTABLISH THE POLICY**

GET EXECUTIVES TO BACK THEIR PROGRAM THROUGH THE LINE ORGANIZATION →

EXECUTIVE

← **GIVE EXECUTIVE BACKING**

HELP TRAINING DIRECTOR PLAN AND OPERATE AN ADEQUATE PROGRAM →

TRAINING

DIRECTOR

← **OPERATE THE PROGRAM**

COACH SUPERVISORS IN THREE SKILLS

INSTRUCTING IMPROVING METHODS LEADING →

SUPERVISORS, FOREMEN, LEADMEN

← **TRAIN SUPERVISORS**

SEE THAT ALL WORKERS PRODUCE
QUICKLY, CORRECTLY, CONSCIENTIOUSLY

WORKERS   WORKERS

The aircraft pictured in the Table of Contents, Chapter, and Index pages is the PBY Catalina built by Consolidated Aircraft Company from 1936 to 1945. The most popular flying boat ever built, the Catalina was designed as a Patrol Bomber but served multiple purposes for many Allied forces during World War II. Vulnerable and slow during daylight operations, the Catalina became a sure-footed bomber when painted a flat black and armed with magnetic anomaly detection gear and torpedoes. This "Black Cat" squadron became the first stealth bomber for the United States Navy in the Pacific theatre of World War II.

MANAGEMENT & SKILLED SUPERVISION

01

T.W.I. PROGRAM AND POLICY

The Training Within Industry Program was established in August 1940 by the National Defense Advisory Commission and was continued under the Office of Production Management and then the War Production Board. By Presidential order on April 18, 1942, Training Within Industry functions were made part of the War Manpower Commission. T. W. I. operates as part of the Bureau of Training.

Management is interested primarily in getting out increased and improved production. Supervision and training are sometimes regarded as separate functions, but they are actually concurrent with management. T. W. I. attempts to get this viewpoint accepted, and T. W. I. work deals exclusively with what management itself can do to train its supervisors.

T. W. I. ADVOCATES

It is recommended that all war production plants give balanced and appropriate attention to the following phases of in–plant training:

1) **Upgrading** of all classes of personnel as their experience and abilities warrant, through planned job progression, job rotation, and intensive supplementary instruction both on and off the job. Each plant should take stock of the talent and experience of its own personnel before employing new men and women.

2) Development of **Production Specialist** through intensive on the job instruction in basic operations.

3) Development of all–round **Skilled Mechanics** through trade apprenticeship, in accordance with Federal standards, separate from production worker training, for the purpose of developing a predetermined, limited number of all–round journeyman mechanics.

4) Development of **Supervisors** through careful selection, assignment of supervisory duties of increasing responsibility, and provision for related organized help through discussions and conferences, under both plant and outside auspices, dealing with methods of instruction, methods of developing better ways of doing a job, methods of improving working relationships, and knowledge of responsibilities.

T. W. I. CONDUCTS

The Training Within Industry Service conducts intensive programs for newly appointed and experienced supervisors and those responsible for in–plant training. There is no authority to enter a plant on any basis other than with management's cooperation. The programs for supervisors require 10 hours of basic training, and 40 hours for training directors.

> *Job Instruction* gives the supervisor practice in how to "break in" men on new jobs.
> *Job Methods* helps the supervisor to simplify and improve methods of doing a job.
> *Job Relations* gives the supervisor practice in how to promote teamwork.

Program Development shows training men how they can develop their own in–plant programs by giving them intensified coaching in a method of planning, operating, and improving plant–wide training programs.

ORGANIZATION

The Training Within Industry Service has a field force with offices in 24 districts throughout the United States and in Hawaii. They are staffed by training and personnel specialists, many of whom are loaned by their companies for part–time or full–time work. Headquarters and field offices have advisers from both management and labor.

The job of getting out war production and of operating essential services is being done by many millions of men and women. The managements of war plants, and other industries such as railroads, and services such as hospitals, depend on their supervisors to get results through these millions of people. The supervisors are the *key* persons in the war production, home–front job.

Since the management responsibilities of supervisors are greater than ever before, the importance of skilled supervision increases daily. At the same time, the difficulties of supervision are mounting—unskilled new workers and changing designs. Many supervisors themselves are new—they have not had time to "grow into their jobs." Under these conditions, every step that management can take to improve the skills of supervision yields important results.

T. W. I. urges management to make the spotting of *all* its training needs the responsibility of a specific person within the organization, and helps him to plan training to meet these needs.

THE SUPERVISOR'S FIVE NEEDS

In order to do the job management expects, the supervisor needs knowledge of his work and of his responsibilities, and must constantly use the skills of instruction, of improving methods, and of working with people.

KNOWLEDGE OF HIS WORK

In order to properly direct the people under his supervision, the supervisor himself must know what doing the particular kind of work involves, what materials and equipment are needed, how the job is done, what standards must be met. Since jobs differ from plant to plant (and even from department to department), only the management knows just what work knowledge is needed by its various supervisors.

KNOWLEDGE OF RESPONSIBILITIES

To the people who work under him, the supervisor *is* management. Unless he clearly knows just what management expects him to pass on to the workers, what plant policies control his actions, and where he fits into the organization, he cannot be an effective supervisor.

Training supervisors in company policies and relationships is an important phase of improving the quality of supervision—and it is a job which each company must carry on for itself, because individual plants are as different as individual persons.

SKILL IN INSTRUCTING

There are over twenty million workers on important jobs which are relatively new to them. There is no time to be wasted on "coming up to production rate," and scrap and rejects must be reduced to a minimum. The supervisor *must* be able to get *a* person to do *a* job, quickly, correctly, and conscientiously.

This problem is common to all supervisors in all plants and can be met through a common approach. Through industrial experience, a 4–step method has evolved. When the supervisor learns this method and uses it, he develops *skill in instructing.* T. W. I. helps management to provide its supervisors with this skill through the Job Instruction program. Management support is essential to insure the acquiring of this skill.

SKILL IN IMPROVING METHODS

Thousands of jobs are being done the way they are done simply because they got started that way. Many people never question the current method—just keep on in the old way. Engineers and technicians develop big improvements, but cannot reach into many operations on single pieces of work which are repeated over and over and which, bulked together, make up the real volume of productive effort.

The development of improvements does not require inventive genius—but it does require the questioning attitude of the supervisor who knows the intimate details. The *skill of improving methods* can be learned. It provides a way for tremendous savings through making more effective use of manpower, machines, and materials. T. W. I. helps management to provide its supervisors with this skill through the Job Methods program. Management support is essential to insure the acquiring of this skill.

SKILL IN WORKING WITH PEOPLE

Full productive effort comes only when the supervisor becomes the leader of his people, when he organizes them into a team and they work well together. In the past, supervisors have developed a *skill in leadership* through experience.

In wartime the situations which cause misunderstandings and grievances have multiplied, and the results of these delays are more serious than ever before. Supervisors must quickly learn to lead their people. T. W. I. helps management to provide its supervisors with this skill through the Job Relations program. Management support is essential to insure the acquiring of this skill.

HOW THE T. W. I. PROGRAMS OPERATE

Training Within Industry experience has proven that results come only when *daily* use is made of what has been acquired through basic training. Accordingly, T. W. I. programs are started in plants only when top management, as a result of spending the time necessary to understand the programs, sponsors the programs, prepares to operate them through the production organization, and demands results.

An important step in operating the T. W. I. programs is informing middle management—the persons who link top executives with operating supervision. They also must understand and accept the programs in order that the supervisors will appreciate the importance of using them.

In any plant, regardless of size, any job requires that some one person be made responsible for getting it done. Getting basic training in the T. W. I. programs accomplished and seeing that supervisors use what they have learned in order that continuing results will be obtained is a real job, and T. W. I. *insists* that the responsibility for this job be definitely assigned.

When these conditions have been met, the Training Within Industry Service makes its techniques available to any eligible establishment (the order of assistance being determined by the priority of importance to the war effort). T. W. I. trains a plant representative to put on the Job Instruction, Job Methods, and Job Relations programs. This preparation of trainers requires one week. T. W. I. provides the training outlines and simple instruction materials.

The trainer conducts a program by putting on five 2–hour sessions for a group of 10 supervisors. These sessions are to be put on daily or on alternate days. Since these programs are depended upon by plants to do a production job for them, T. W. I. urges managements to schedule these sessions during working hours, at plant expense.

In all three of the programs, the first session is devoted to the exposition of a 4–step method for supervisors to use. The other four sessions (8 hours out of the 10) are spent by the supervisors in practicing on their own problems.

If a plant is too small to be able to have a trainer from its own staff (in general, this means plants with less than 50 supervisors to be trained), T. W. I. will arrange for an outside trainer who can be compensated for his time through state vocational funds.

After the basic training phase of any one of these programs is started, T. W. I. representatives help the plant to set up procedures to give sustained support to the programs in order that they will be used and results obtained continuously.

Union stewards are eligible for participation in the Job Relations program, either in sessions put on by union trainers under union sponsorship, or as members of plant groups made up of both supervisors and stewards.

THE JOB INSTRUCTION PROGRAM

When a supervisor has to break–in a man on a new job, he is interested in having him come up to quality and quantity requirements of production as quickly as possible, in avoiding accidents which will injure the worker, in avoiding damage to machines and equipment, and in spoiling as little work as possible.

In order to accomplish this, the supervisor needs to get ready to instruct; he must:

> *Have a time table:*
>> how much skill you expect him to have, by what date?
>
> *Break down the job:*
>> list important steps.
>>
>> pick out the key points.
>
> *Have everything ready:*
>> the right equipment, materials, and supplies.
>
> *Have the workplace properly arranged:*
>> just as the worker will be expected to keep it.

These "get–ready" points provide the basis on which the 4–step method of instruction is started:

STEP 1 PREPARE THE WORKER
- Put him at ease.
- State the job and find out what he already knows about it.
- Get him interested in learning job.
- Place in correct position.

STEP 2 PRESENT THE OPERATION
- Tell, show, and illustrate one **Important Step** at a time.
- Stress each **Key Point.**
- Instruct clearly, completely, and patiently, but no more than he can master.

STEP 3 TRY OUT PERFORMANCE
- Have him do the job—correct errors.
- Have him explain each **Key Point** to you as he does the job again.
- Make sure he understands.
- Continue until **You** know **He** knows.

STEP 4 FOLLOW UP
- Put him on his own. Designate to whom he goes for help.
- Check frequently. Encourage questions.
- Taper off extra coaching and close follow–up.

Throughout the 10 hours, the trainers stress: *If the worker hasn't learned, the instructor hasn't taught.*

When supervisors *use* the Job Instruction steps, break–in time is reduced, accidents decrease, and scrap loss falls.

TYPICAL RESULTS OF USE OF JOB INSTRUCTION

STEEL COMPANY—"In the past it has taken *6 weeks* to break in a man or woman in handling a traveling overhead crane. After J. I. training of instructors in how to break in people on a crane operation by following a breakdown sheet of the job, it now takes *6 1/2 days*. This includes the proper operator maintenance of the crane."

ELECTRIC MANUFACTURING COMPANY—"One month after the J. I. program was started, reject tickets were reduced about *50%* in two departments with 2,500 workers."

SHIPYARD— "A crew, originally of *85* men, now of *70* (49 of them women), is turning out *10%* more work than the original and larger crew did. Better method of training through J. I., effected this result."

BRASS COMPANY—"On one operation where 9,600 pieces were run per 8 hours, there was an average of *1,770 pieces of scrap*. A J. I. key point reduced the scrap to *25* pieces, and further application of J. I. reduced this to *5* pieces in *20,000*."

THE JOB METHODS PROGRAM

Materials are growing scarcer, machinery is difficult to replace, and manpower is critical. Better ways to use available materials, machines, and manpower are developed when supervisors use the Job Methods technique:

STEP 1 BREAK DOWN THE JOB
1) List all details of the job exactly as done by the present method.
2) Be sure details include all:
    • Material handling.
    • Machine work.
    • Hand work.

STEP 2 QUESTION EVERY DETAIL
1) Use these types of questions:
    • WHY is it necessary?
    • WHAT is its purpose?
    • WHERE should it be done?
    • WHEN should it be done?
    • WHO is best qualified to do it?
    • HOW is the "best way" to do it?
2) Also question the:
    Materials, machines, equipment, tools, product design, layout, safety, housekeeping.

STEP 3 DEVELOP THE NEW METHOD
1) **Eliminate** unnecessary details.
2) **Combine** details when practical.

3) **Rearrange** for better sequence.
4) **Simplify** all necessary details:
   - To make the work easier and safer.
   - Pre–position materials, tools and equipment at the best places in the proper work area.
   - Use gravity–feed hoppers and drop–delivery chutes.
   - Let both hands do useful work.
   - Use jigs and fixtures instead of hands, for holding work.
5) Work out your idea with others.
6) Write up your proposed new method.

STEP 4 APPLY THE NEW METHOD
1) Sell your proposal to your "boss."
2) Sell the new method to the operators.
3) Get final approval of all concerned on safety, quality, quantity, cost.
4) Put the new method to work. Use it until a better way is developed.
5) Give credit where credit is due.

American industry today is the result of improvements. Many of these improvements have been made by specialists, or else by someone who had one "flash" idea that worked. This Job Methods technique stimulates *every* supervisor to look critically at all the jobs he directs not just once, but repeatedly, as a part of his supervisory job.

TYPICAL RESULTS OF USE OF JOB METHODS

AIRCRAFT PLANT—"An average of *12 hours* per plane was being lost in the installation and adjustment of the door–locking mechanism. Workers designed a new lock, accepted by engineering and management, with the result that perfect installation and adjustment can be made in about *20 minutes.*"

CEMENT COMPANY—"An improved method for feeding cement sacks into a cleaner saved *35 miles* of walking per day, 70 women employees affected."

WAREHOUSE—"In the operation of wrapping 100–pound to 600–pound rolls of duck, a J. M. improvement resulted in a saving of *48%* in man–hours, a reduction in the department affected from *1,008* hours to *528* hours per 48–hour week, and eliminated one fork lift and truck. This improvement also eliminated skin infections from handling, and results in savings at the annual rate of *$300,000* in labor and material."

CAN COMPANY—"(1) By a new method for testing cans, the girl now doing the job can handle *3* more machines and still have *2* hours left out of 8. (2) In making solder, during busy times one man had to lift twice (once up 4 feet on to a truck and again off the truck into a smelter) a total of *8,000 pounds*, or *4 tons*, of material per day. By a new method, all this lifting is eliminated. (3) A new method of handling and cutting dunnage lumber results in a *25%* saving in cost and eliminates *6* trips of *900* feet each way per carload of cans."

THE JOB RELATIONS PROGRAM

The supervisor can avoid many problems in his department if he builds a foundation of good relations. T. W. I. stresses these fundamentals:

Let each worker know how he is getting along.
> Figure out what you expect of him. Point out ways to improve.

Give credit when due.
> Look for extra or unusual performance. Tell him while "it's hot."

Tell people in advance about changes that will affect them.
> Tell them WHY if possible.
> Get them to accept the change.

Make best use of each person's ability.
> Look for ability not now being used. Never stand in a man's way.

People Must Be Treated As Individuals.

Applying these foundations is not, however, enough. Because problems do arise, the supervisor must be able to handle them before they seriously affect production or grow to larger proportions. The problem–solving technique is:

DETERMINE OBJECTIVE

STEP 1 PREPARE THE WORKER
- Review the record.
- Find out what rules and plant customs apply. Talk with individuals concerned.
- Get opinions and feelings.

Be sure you have the whole story.

STEP 2 WEIGH AND DECIDE
- Fit the facts together.
- Consider their bearing on each other. What possible actions are there?
- Check practices and policies.
- Consider objective and effect on individual, group, and production.

Don't jump at conclusions.

STEP 3 TAKE ACTION
- Are you going to handle this yourself?
- Do you need help in handling?
- Should you refer this to your supervisor?
- Watch the timing of your action.

Don't pass the buck.

STEP 4 CHECK RESULTS
- How soon will you follow up?
- How often will you need to check?
- Watch for changes in output, attitudes, and relationships.

Did your action help production?

TYPICAL RESULTS OF USE OF JOB RELATIONS

COAL MINE—"As a direct result of Job Relations, the output of coal has increased 120 cars per week (480 tons of coal)."

STEEL COMPANY—"Complaint cases to management have dropped 54% since J. R. was started. Grievance committee meets now on an average of three times a month; formerly it was at least three times per week."

RADIO PLANT—"Since the Job Relations program has been in effect, about 6 weeks, employee complaints or grievances have been reduced 97%, or from 30 per month to 1 per month."

FOOD PLANT—"Most of the problems that used to come to management are now handled by the foremen themselves. Foremen have increased confidence. The foremen are noticeably careful in making a decision to be sure they are within the practices and policies of the company so that they will be supported by their superiors."

MEETING THE PLANT'S OVERALL TRAINING NEEDS

The majority of T. W. I. time is spent in the field of supervision but, as stated, T. W. I. programs are not started in a plant until management has indicated its definite intent to stress their use by giving the responsibility for training direction or coordination to a specific person.

T. W. I. provides to management assistance for this training man through 4–day Program Development institutes in which the man learns and uses a 4–step method of meeting production problems through training.

STEP 1 SPOT A PRODUCTION PROBLEM
- Get supervisors and workers to tell about their current problems.
- Uncover problems by reviewing records—performance, cost, turnover, rejects, accidents.
- Anticipate problems resulting from changes to the organization, production, or policies.
- Analyze this evidence.
- Identify training needed.

Tackle one specific need at a time.

STEP 2 DEVELOP A SPECIFIC PLAN
- WHO will be trained?
- WHAT content?
- WHO can help determine?
- HOW can it be done best?
- WHO should do the training?
- WHEN should it be done—how long will it take?
- WHERE should it be done?

Watch for relation of this plan to other current training plans and programs.

STEP 3 GET PLAN INTO ACTION

- Stress to management evidence of need—use facts and figures.
- Present the expected results.
- Discuss plan—content and methods.
- Submit timetable for plan.
- Train those who do the training.
- Secure understanding and acceptance by those affected.
- Fix responsibility for continuing use.

Be sure management participates.

STEP 4 CHECK RESULTS

- How can results be checked? Against what evidence?
- What results will be looked for?
- Is management being informed—how?
- Is the plan being followed?
- How is it being kept in use?
- Are any changes necessary?

Is the Plan Helping Production?

The *Institute* is scheduled as two consecutive days during which the members practice the method, using material drawn from many industries. Then they return, after one week, for work on their own plans which they have meanwhile developed. Throughout, T. W. I. stresses that:

The *Line* organization has the responsibility for making continuing use of the knowledge and skills acquired through training as a regular part of the operating job.

The *Staff* provides plans and technical "know how," and does some things *for* but usually works *through* the line organization.

THE TRAINING WITHIN INDUSTRY PROGRAM

02

The Office of Production Management has established this service for defense contractors and sub–contractors to assist them in meeting the increasing needs for skilled workers and supervisors.

The underlying **purpose** of this activity is:

To assist defense industries to meet their manpower needs by training within industry each worker to make the fullest use of his best skill up to the maximum of his individual ability, thereby enabling production to keep pace with defense demands.

Based upon types of requests for assistance which have been received from industry, the **problem** of providing the kinds of skill needed divides into three parts:

1) INVENTORY OF PRESENT SKILLS. This should include those employed below their greatest usefulness as well as the unemployed. Various national and local governmental agencies, and other cooperating groups, are at work gathering this information, but each plant should also take stock of the talent and experience of its own employees and make internal adjustments before employing new men.

2) TRAINING OUTSIDE OF INDUSTRY. This includes pre–employment instruction and related supplementary instruction. This part of the program is being provided for by public and private vocational and trade schools and by engineering colleges, but it is of such vital interest to industry that the closest kind of cooperation must be continuously maintained with them.

National Youth Administration, Work Projects Administration, and Civilian Conservation Corps also offer opportunities for pre–employment work experience making for better preparation for work in defense industries.

It is of utmost importance that the industries served participate actively with the schools in setting up entrance standards, so that all who complete the school training will be acceptable for employment. It is also important that the numbers of persons trained be not greatly in excess of the needs of the industries served. Industry can well afford to supply some of its first–class employees to schools as teachers. Some of their retired employees may be excellent instructors. Industrial management can also assist these other agencies in making their services increasingly useful to industry by constant consultation regarding job requirements.

3) TRAINING WITHIN INDUSTRY. This particularly deals with industry's own training responsibilities and is the area in which the efforts of this activity are concentrated. It is accomplished through upgrading of all classes of personnel as their experience and abilities warrant, through planned job progression, job rotation, and intensive supplementary instruction both on and off the job. The conclusions of various recent conferences confirm experience that this training includes three phases:

  a) Development of *production specialists* through intensive on the job instruction, according to basic operations.

  b) Development of all–round *skilled mechanics* through trades apprenticeship, in accordance with federal standards, separate from production worker training, for the purpose of developing a pre–determined, limited number of all–round journeymen mechanics.

  c) Development of *supervisors* through careful selection, assignment of supervisory duties of increasing responsibility, and provision for related organized help through discussions and conferences under both plant and outside auspices.

Technical and other management assistants must be developed also.

This organization renders specific ADVISORY ASSISTANCE to defense industries in inaugurating programs which they carry on within their own plants at their own expense. The availability of this service is widely known, but is not compulsory. There is no authority to go into a plant on any basis other than at management's request.

Four general types of assistance apply in most cases and are being adapted to fit the various conditions in each specific plant.

1. Help in the analysis of the training needs.

2. Aid in setting up a program within the plant to meet its needs.

3. Experience of other employers who have let similar problems is made available through headquarters and field clearance.

4. Availability of the services of tax–supported government agencies, such as state and federal employment service, vocational and trade schools, engineering colleges, N.Y.A., C.C.C., W.P.A. made known to plant managements so that the fullest use may be made of them. Only through interpreting the needs of industry to these agencies, and their closest coordination, can they furnish the most effective preemployment education and pre–employment experience as well as related instruction for employed workers.

A COUNTRY–WIDE ORGANIZATION to assist individual defense manufacturers in the solution of their training problems operates through 22 field offices of the Training within Industry branch of the O.P.M. Labor Division.

In charge of each is a District Representative who is the direct agent of headquarters at Washington. Borrowed from industry, he was selected for his background in production and industrial relations. In most districts he is supported by an Assistant Representative.

Associated with the District Representatives in each district are four Advisers, two who represent Management and two representing Labor. With a broad background in their respective fields, the Advisers promote helpful relationships and stimulate wider interest in the advantages of training in the plant.

The personal service that Training within Industry renders to the individual manufacturer is performed most often by one of several Consultants. They are part of the district organization and are members of the industrial community they serve. Consultants bring to their tasks extensive experience in the fields of management, production, and personnel, and have an understanding of local factors. Their services are available on request to the District Representative.

Activities of field organizations are directed from headquarters at Washington.

15

THE HEADQUARTERS' STAFF consists of the Director, Associate Director, Assistant Directors, and specialists with broad experience in the training problems of industry. The staff is assisted by an Advisory Committee composed of six representatives of Labor and six of Management. Technical Consultants, responsible for the successful administration of training in industry, complete the staff.

Both the headquarters and district offices are described, along with listings of personnel, in Organization and Personnel Bulletin #1–A. The territory served by each office is shown by a map included in the bulletin.

EXPANDING THE MANAGERIAL ORGANIZATION

03

Expanding the organization in the initial stages is a simple problem. However, when expansion is required to the point, where as one company executive expresses it, "the supervisory organization is stretched beyond the elastic limit", the problem becomes crucial. Further expansion and use of inexperienced men may mean failure of certain operation, or departments. It may mean the tie-up of the whole plant, high scrap losses and serious difficulties in meeting production and quality standards.

The following plans have been found successful in many companies, and are such that they may be adapted to most any organization. There are many companies to which these will not be new.

C. R. Dooley, Director
Training Within Industry

PLANNING FOR EXPANSION

The following four steps are ones normally encountered when expanding an organization. The plans there under are basic enough to be adapted to various situations.

1. GIVE EACH PRESENT SUPERVISOR MORE RESPONSIBILITY

When production volume increases, of course, the first obvious method of handling it is to give each present supervisor more responsibility, i.e., more men, more equipment, more floor space, and often more authority. Occasionally sections or departments are combined and placed under one supervisor where previously there were two or more supervisors.

2. SELECT MEN FROM PRESENT SUPERVISORY FORCE TO FILL POSITIONS OF NEW OR GREATER RESPONSIBILITIES

Usually, there is a limited number of qualified supervisors from which men may be selected, competent to take full charge of new departments, new plants or to assume newly created functions.

Immediate attention to replacement and the preparation of understudies is essential. In fact, many executives find it practical to draw an organization chart, and to place under each strategic position the names of several men who could fill such position, in the order of their availability and competence. On one or two successive charts, plans are drawn showing how the organization would be expanded and men shifted under anticipated contingencies. Thus the department head, General Superintendent or Works Manager, may specifically plan his understudies and moves, and avoid "getting in a pinch" when faced with a large order or an important expansion. Where there is a Personnel or Industrial Relations Department, this department can be particularly helpful by developing such confidential charts and plans and submitting them to line executives for suggestions and approval.

This procedure also makes it possible to give the maximum amount of organized training to understudies and men who are to be shifted or promoted. The personnel officer, in collaboration with operating executives can then prepare job rotation, progression and observation training, and institute organized instruction in the fundamentals of supervision and technical information.

3. SELECT AND TRAIN BEGINNING SUPERVISORS

When it becomes necessary, *new* supervisors must be selected and appointed. Each company management shows the best source in each instance, whether from the ranks of workers, engineers, technicians, or others.

Experience proves conclusively that intelligence, personality, vitality, and other leadership abilities should outweigh technical or trade ability when such selections are made. Of course, there are some functions where technical knowledge is essential, and in such cases it must be recognized.

The following approach represents the principal features of a successful plan now being widely used, by which properly chosen appointees are developed into quite competent supervisors in 8 or 10 weeks.

a) Assign the new appointee to elementary supervisory work 2 to 3 weeks

It has been found that special training for a new supervisor in the principles of supervision, labor policies and similar fields, is more effective AFTER he has had a taste of supervisory responsibility. For the first two or three weeks, therefore, he should be given supervision of a normal experienced group of workmen where there are no exceptional problems of production, discipline or worker training. During this first assignment, he should be made responsible for routine duties, such as—shop orders, time tickets, material ordering, work assignment, routine production, quality, and schedule control. He should be closely guided and coached in these matters by an experienced supervisor. He should NOT be thrown into problems or controversies on wage payment, grievances, discipline, employee selection, transfer or dismissal, maintenance, cost analyses and like questions.

b) Give the new supervisor intensive instruction—1 to 2 weeks

Take the beginning supervisor (in groups of 3 or 4, up to 12) off the job 4 hours a day for 15 to 18 consecutive days or full time for 6 to 10 days. Give him concentrated instruction in the principal features of his new supervisory job. This will prepare him to deal more confidently with difficult situations as they arise. Otherwise it may be months before he encounters them and learns how to deal with them through costly trial and error. Discussion of typical operating cases, problems and questions should be lifted directly out of job situations. An experienced training specialist, using suitable training quarters, can thus help beginning supervisors to acquire much of the knowledge and judgment which would otherwise require months or years to gain.

This intensive instruction should be scheduled about as follows:

Supervisory job planning	6 hours
Theory and practice of instructing workers	48 hours
Personnel responsibilities	6 hours
Labor policies and procedures	6 hours

This plan particularly requires the careful attention of management, training specialist and foreman alike. While it is difficult to take the new man off the job, companies find that the long term advantage outweighs the short term inconvenience. After such instruction, men are able to accept full responsibility sooner and make fewer mistakes in the meantime.

c) Assign the new supervisor to more difficult and responsible work—4 to 6 weeks

The new supervisor now has begun to have a basis for judgment and should be placed in a position where he is responsible for a normal working group including some inexperienced workers. He should have contact with the full range of supervisory problems, and under experienced coaching, should be given responsibility for them just as rapidly as he is able to handle them properly.

In some situations, it may be found at this stage that it will expedite production if the new supervisor is given the special assignment of instructing new workers. It is sometimes advantageous to use him on such work for several weeks or several months.

d) Put the new supervisor "on his own"

At this stage, the new supervisor may be given normal line responsibility under normal supervisory guidance and share in whatever staff meetings, supervisory conference, or other organized aids are available.

4. DEVELOP A RESERVE OR POOL OF POTENTIAL SUPERVISORS

Future needs for supervisors should be anticipated and a pool of qualified men developed. Many men are broadening their outlook and scope of knowledge through out–of–hour study in university extension, correspondence schools, company classes, and through individual study of company products and producing methods. Often among such men there are excellent candidates for beginning supervisory jobs.

It has been found advantageous to make arrangements to use an outside service—state university or state vocational education department—for a course in "Foremanship" adapted to their particular needs. Under such outside auspices, enrollees do not expect immediate recognition by the company and yet the company has a pool of interested and partially trained potential supervisors from which to draw.

When pre–supervisory training is set up and offered by a company and open to voluntary enrollment, men who take the training will expect recognition. This is true in spite of the fact that no job offers are made or implied, yet their disappointment is a serious morale factor when they are not selected for supervisory positions.

STRENGTHENING THE MANAGERIAL ORGANIZATION

04

Helping managerial personnel to meet its operating responsibilities is the key to the success of an organization. It is also the key to the training of new workers and to the upgrading of present workers. Always it is the key to the maintenance of high morale throughout the work force, which represents the very foundation of the industrial defense program.

The recommended practices outlined herein, represent successful programs in many companies throughout the country.

C. R. Dooley, Director
Training Within Industry

UNDERLYING POLICY

Planned development is the key point in considering the building of a strong executive and supervisory force. In such planning many companies stress one or two features and feel that these will build a strong managerial group. Some maintain a favorable salary scale; others have a liberal retirement plan; some stress periodic rating; others pursue excellent training programs; still others emphasize the close personal relationship between upper and lower levels of supervision.

Individually these features are sound, of course, but no one or two of them are sufficient. The full range of factors affecting supervisors and executives must be given attention and action if a company is to be assured of a strong, energetic, and cooperative managerial force.

Typical of the many examples sharing the necessity of attention to all aspects of this problem are the following:

Foremen are not likely to do their best work in meeting schedules and reducing costs if they are held responsible for delays and costs over which they have no control.

A foreman finds it difficult to be genuinely helpful to a worker who has a wage question if he has a question regarding his own compensation.

Any executive or supervisor is not likely to keep close touch with his group if he is able to see his own superior but once or twice a month.

Many an executive or supervisor stays with his company because the salary is satisfactory, but uses but a portion of his real capacity because his area of responsibility is not clear, his relationship with his boss not cordial, or he is a victim of internal politics.

Examples such as the foregoing, illustrate why sound and farsighted management policy is so important, and why such policy, even when it has been formulated, does not serve its intended purpose unless all members of the managerial group understand it and know their specific responsibility in carrying it out.

SOUND PRACTICES

The following fundamentals—already well known—represent some of the principal practices which build a strong managerial force.

SELECTION

1. Select executives and supervisors on a basis of leadership qualities, and not alone on job knowledge and job skills.

An important aid at the time of selection is the preparation of a written position description, setting forth clearly the duties and results expected of the incumbent.

2. Prepare a chart of the whole organization. Discuss it with all executives and supervisors. See that each man understands the functions and relationships of the various units and particularly his own place and function in the organization.

3. See that all members of the executive and supervisory group understand the company's policies, particularly, industrial relations policies.

A growing number of companies are reducing to writing their basic policies, both to clarify just what the policies are, and to assure that everyone in the company understands them.

4. See that each executive and supervisor is given sufficient authority to carry out the responsibility assigned to him.

5. Give such organized aid and training to the executive and supervisory force as is appropriate and will be helpful on current problems.

This is an important point representing a program in itself. Bulletin 4–B is devoted specifically to how such aid and training may be given. It is important to note that a well rounded plan for Strengthening the Managerial Organization requires attention to the twelve points mentioned herein, plus the amplification of this section in Bulletin 4–B.

6. Plan transfers and rotations as well as promotions. Some companies make transfers and rotations for the express purpose of developing and **rounding-out** individual executives and supervisors and not solely to fill positions after a need has arisen. They find that competent men in widely differing fields can "trade jobs", not only without impairment to operations, but with distinct profit to the men and to the jobs. Fresh and unprejudiced points of view toward the new jobs usually result in outstanding improvements. It is not uncommon for executives with 25 years service to have had ten to fifteen different positions. The resultant competence, breadth of knowledge and judgment is a major factor in the success of companies pursuing this plan.

7. Encourage professional development. Membership in engineering, management, accounting, sales and other professional societies, and appropriate participation therein is encouraged by many companies. Foremanship too, is a field of growing professional interest.

STATUS AND PAY

8. Give supervisors all the privileges of salaried employees, plus whatever additional privileges are appropriate in each local situation, i.e., parking space, desk equipment, lockers and other symbols of status.

9. See that supervisors, particularly foremen, are "in the know," i.e., trust them, give them actual departmental profit and loss figures, not just non–hour reports. Have them review (solicit their suggestions when

appropriate) and see that they understand any plan that *involves* them such as:

Job classification	Change in cost reports
Wage payment plans	New inspection plan
Contemplated purchase of new equipment	Union agreement, grievance procedures and settlement
Rating plan concerning themselves or workers	New layout of department
New production standards or quality standards	Plans for upgrading workers and supervisors

Above all, see that foremen are informed as to any new general company policy or provision *before* such information is released to workers. Examples: new plant rules; sick pay plan; provisions relating to military training and service; new union contract, agreement or procedure; new defense contract received; wage and hour law rulings.

10. Pay supervisors not only the going salary rate, but a rate appropriately above those supervised.

11. Pay all supervisors on a salary basis, i.e., all who give their full time to directing the work of others. Lead men, working foremen or those whose supervisory function deals only with assigning work and helping maintain production schedules, maybe exceptions.

During periods of temporarily slack operation, do not reduce supervisors to an hourly rate unless such a period is prolonged and it becomes necessary to demote them to hourly rated jobs. Until this action is taken as a last resort, have them work part–time and pay them proportionately, but maintain them on the *salary roll*.

12. Give appropriate salary increases based upon performance. Avoid being influenced by the many personal relationships that obtain in every organization.

In many companies it is the accepted policy that the development of a foreman, superintendent or works manager is just as important as the development of a product, plant or policy. Just as much attention is given to planning the one as to the other. In planning the development of managerial personnel, a great many factors are considered. They embrace all the day–to–day practices and influences in the company which make for sound growth, development and prudent management.

HOW TO IMPROVE JOB RELATIONS

05

In these times, for maximum production, machines and materials are not enough. We need the individual skills and the maximum cooperation of every man and woman who is at work turning out what our armed forces and civilian workers have to have.

You know how important it is not to have any lost production because of misunderstandings on the job, or because people do not realize the vital part they have in the war effort, or because some one is slowed down on his job by things that happened off the job.

Experienced supervisors who have demonstrated their ability to "work well with people" have developed a special skill. You can acquire this skill. By making use of it, you can be more sure of meeting your production requirements.

This is the time; and the place is right where you are!

C. R. Dooley, Director
Training Within Industry Service

EVERYDAY PROBLEMS

Does anyone in your department ever refuse to do some particular job? Or, maybe, even quit his job? Do you have any people who are discouraged or who make other people dissatisfied?

Are there any changes being made in your plant—in how you work, what you do—in the people you work with?

Does everyone come to work regularly, or are you ever held up by absenteeism? And do you ever find you are by–passed by people who go over your head to your own boss?

All job relations problems don't come up at once, but they do occur, and management *does* hold supervisors responsible for handling such problems.

The supervisor today needs a high degree of skill to handle his own problems. But, as part of the skill, first of all, he needs a strong foundation for good relationships with the people whose work he directs.

THE FOUNDATION OF GOOD RELATIONS

You do not produce a ton of steel, build a single jeep—it is the people you supervise who turn out production. The supervisor needs to remember constantly that *results come through people.*

There are certain basic principles which are foundations in establishing and maintaining good relations between you and those whose work you direct. Always remember to:

Let each worker know how he is getting along.

Give credit when due.

Tell people in advance about changes that will effect them. Make best use of each person's ability.

These principles apply to all workers, and they do not represent actions which are to be taken only once or at rare intervals. Constantly following them in day–to–day operation will pay dividends.

LET EACH WORKER KNOW HOW HE IS GETTING ALONG

It is important to keep people posted on how they are measuring up against what is expected of them. The "everything is all right unless I tell you so" philosophy does not fit into modern supervision. The man who is doing all right should be told so. And it is often *more* important to check the person who is just beginning to skid. If you have to say "you've been slipping for quite a while," you know what the worker will feel—"why didn't you tell me sooner?"

GIVE CREDIT WHEN DUE

The worker and the department deserve to know when their efforts have contributed to an accomplishment. Recognition of good work or faithful performance makes it easier to get extra effort again. *You* like to get proper credit yourself.

TELL PEOPLE IN ADVANCE ABOUT CHANGES THAT WILL AFFECT THEM

It is not always possible for you to let a worker "in" on all decisions which affect him, but he can and should always be given the chance to "have his say.' If you give the reason for changes before they are made, you will avoid many misunderstandings.

MAKE BEST USE OF EACH PERSON'S ABILITY

Everyone likes to feel, particularly in war time, that he is working at his highest level of skill and ability. Take advantage of special interest in kinds of work, and give each person as much, and as responsible, work as he can handle.

TREATING PEOPLE AS INDIVIDUALS

While these foundations apply to all people, you cannot let it go at "treating them all alike." No one wants to be known simply as a time–card number or as "the new man"—neither you nor those you supervise. We are all different. What happens to one operator off the job makes him different from his partner on the same job. Each of us wants to be known for his own personal characteristics. There are things that you feel are important to you as an individual. You must remember other individuals feel the same.

Applying these foundations of good worker–supervisor relations will not guarantee smooth operation for you, but will prevent many misunderstandings.

However, there are other things which *you must consider.* You need to know each individual employee and what is important to him You need to know your people for everyday operation of your department, and you particularly need this information when you have a difficult situation to handle as a job relations problem.

HOW TO HANDLE A PROBLEM

Because changes do occur, and problems do arise, you need to have skill in handling the situations which are within your responsibility. Often you are on the spot and you feel you must do something immediately. Hasty action may mean that you have a more difficult situation to handle later. You always must stop to consider just what you are trying to accomplish. These steps should then be considered as the outline for action.

1) Get the facts—be sure you have the whole story.
2) Weigh and decide—don't jump at conclusions.
3) Take action—don't pass the buck.
4) Check results—did your action help production?

1. GET THE FACTS

Problems may come up because of something that happens at the moment, but you need to get the whole background. Some of it will be made up of facts about the employee—his age, length of service, and experience on this job.

You will need, of course, to take into consideration both the plant rules and just "the way things are done here."

Remember in getting the facts you may think you know the person quite well, but if you classify him as a "good Police or a "chronic kicker," you are not really looking at an individual person. You must regard him as a person who is different from his work partner and from every other person in the department, in every single aspect whether by a very slight or a very great degree.

As a supervisor, you must know what that man thinks and feels about himself and the people around him. Find out what the man wants—is he able or willing to express it—and what does he think should be done? and *why*? The experienced supervisor knows that he must also consider such other factors as health and working conditions which may be affecting the man.

If more than one person is involved, you must go through the same fact–finding steps for each person. Before you can plan what to do, you must be sure you really have the whole story.

2. WEIGH AND DECIDE

All these facts must be assembled and considered together. They will suggest various "possible actions" which you must check against your objective, and the effect on the individual, the group, and production. When all the factors are brought together, fitted in, and considered in the light of their relations to each other, many times the right answer almost "jumps out." The wise thing to do becomes clearer.

Certainly you, the man on the spot, are in the best place to know the right thing to do, for you have the most complete picture of the assembled facts. If you jump to conclusions, you make poor use of your strategic position. When you act without evaluating the whole situation you are likely to have more difficult problems to handle later.

3. TAKE ACTION

While jumping to conclusions is a poor way to handle supervisory problems, putting off action may be equally unfortunate. A supervisor cannot "pass the buck" or he, himself, will be by–passed.

However, it is not "passing the buck" to recognize after full consideration of the problem that there are some situations which you cannot handle yourself. You also make a decision and take action when you size up a situation as one on which you need help, or recognize one which is not within your own job to handle and see that it is passed on to the person who does have the responsibility and authority.

In any action, timing must be considered—the wrong "time" can make it the wrong thing to do.

4. CHECK RESULTS

You must determine whether your action worked. If it did not, you must re–examine the whole situation and attempt to find what of importance you overlooked. Checking the results of action is necessary in every situation because conditions change, and what worked with one individual will not necessarily work with another.

"GOOD" SUPERVISION

One of the hardest parts of your job will be that of giving consideration to the importance of people in a problem situation and knowing what is important to each individual person. This is not simply a matter of determining what is right or wrong, or deciding what is just or unjust, but is a practical approach to effective supervision. It may be thought to take too much time but day–by–day use of this skill in dealing with people will save you time in the long run.

If you know your people well enough to build them into a smooth group you will be playing an important part in war production.

HOW TO IMPROVE JOB METHODS

0 6

You know materials are growing scarcer. Machines are difficult to get or replace. And manpower is getting to be a critical issue. A big part of the answer is to develop better ways of doing the work you supervise with the manpower, machines, and materials *now available*.

Perhaps you worked out a better way to do one of the jobs you supervise to-day. If so, you made an important contribution to victory. But are you working out better methods *every day*?

Here is a Plan that will help you develop those *better job methods **now***. It will help you to produce greater quantities, of quality products, in less time.

31

The principles are not new. The Plan was worked out in its present practical and usable form by industrial men who are facing the same problems as yourself. Use this plan every day. Use it on *every* job you supervise. The more you use it, the more opportunities you will find to put it to work.

Today, the need is to improve *job methods* to help do the biggest production job in history! The need is for you to make *more* improvements and to make them *now!*

C. R. Dooley, Director
Training within Industry Service

JOB IMPROVEMENT HAS ALWAYS BEEN A PART OF YOUR JOB

You are looking for improvements every day. This is, and always has been, a part of your job. Continued improvement of basic ideas has made our country what it is. Think of the automobiles of 15 years ago. Compare them with the cars of today. Remember the radio of a few years ago? And the airplanes? And the rifles—and guns—in fact, thousands of modern pieces of fighting equipment that were unknown a few years ago? All this progress is the result of improvement. Some of it is improvement in design to be sure. But much of it is improvement in the *methods* of production. You may not be able to do much about basic design, but you *can* do something about the production methods.

GO AFTER THE "SMALL THINGS"

Look for the *hundreds* of *small things* you can improve. Don't try to plan a whole new department layout—or go after a big new installation of new equipment. There isn't time for these major items. Look for improvements on existing jobs, with your *present* equipment.

THE "WAY" YOU MAKE IMPROVEMENTS IS OF FIRST IMPORTANCE

Go back in your memory as a workman.

Remember the time you "put up" with a job because it was awkward and caused you needless trouble and worry? Remember the "better way" you finally worked out which would have made it safer and easier to do? Remember how you wanted to tell your boss about your idea but he wasn't the kind of a fellow who was easy to talk to, and you never mentioned it to him?

Or perhaps, you remember the time when the boss "sprung" *his* new method on you and you had a pretty tough time "swallowing" it.

You will *never* forget the time when the boss "had an idea" and asked you for *your* opinion about it, and how you made several good improvements in his plan and how pleased you were.

Then go back over your experience as a supervisor.

Remember the time you put a new idea "up to the boss?" It was rather poorly worked out and he found a "bug" in your plan right off? And you didn't propose any more.

Remember the time you really had a good plan, but you neglected to get some of your fellow supervisors and engineers "in on it" and the plan fell flat?

Then, of course, you will NEVER forget the "better way" you worked out, that was put into effect and that did work. You still can feel the satisfaction that it gave you.

HOW TO IMPROVE JOB METHODS

BETTER JOB METHODS are needed NOW—desperately so—but there is a RIGHT WAY to make them. Here is the plan. It has worked in thousands of cases, and in practically every kind of industry. There are FOUR STEPS to follow. No one step can be omitted. No one step is more important than the other.

STEP 1 BREAK DOWN THE JOB

1) List *all* details of the job *exactly* as done by the Present Method.

2) Be sure details include all:

- Material Handling
- Machine Work
- Hand Work

Take any job, take the first one you see in your department.

Just "start right in"—jot down on a sheet of paper every *detail* as it happens. Do this right at the job. Don't try to do it back at your desk. You'll overlook something if you do.

Don't be secretive or mysterious about it. Tell your workers what you are doing. Be frank and open about the listing of details.

STEP 2 QUESTION EVERY DETAIL

1) Use these types of questions:
- WHY is it necessary?
- WHAT is its purpose?
- WHERE should it be done?
- WHEN should it be done?
- WHO is best qualified to do it?
- HOW is "the best way" to do it?

2) Also question the:

Materials, Machines, Equipment, Tools, Product Design, Layout, Work Place, Safety, Housekeeping.

Just start down your sheet of details. Start questioning each one. You won't get far, usually, until some improvements will occur to you.

Perhaps a *"better way"* will "flash" into your mind. Hold this "new idea" temporarily and question EVERY DETAIL on your list before you start to "dope out" the better way. If you stop to work your "flash," you may help only *a part* of the job, and overlook a *broader* or *more useful* improvement.

STEP 3 DEVELOP THE NEW METHOD

1) **Eliminate** unnecessary details.
2) **Combine** details when practical.
3) **Rearrange** details for better sequence.
4) **Simplify** all necessary details,

   a) Make the work *easier* and *safer.*
   b) Pre–position materials, tools and equipment at the best places in the proper work area.
   c) Use gravity–feed hoppers and drop–delivery chutes when practical.
   d) Let both hands do useful work.
   e) Use jigs and fixtures instead of hands, for holding work.

5) WORK OUT your idea WITH others.
6) Write up your proposed new method.

   Eliminating unnecessary details prevents waste of materials and manpower.

   Combining and rearranging overcome "back tracking" and double handling.

   Simplifying makes the job easier and safer to do.

   Be sure to get all those concerned "in on" your idea from the start. Don't work out the new method and "spring it" on your people. This applies to your boss, your associates, and *particularly to your workers.* The best way of all is to work out your idea with them. Make them *a part of it.*

STEP 4 APPLY THE NEW METHOD

1) *Sell* your proposal to the *boss.*
2) *Sell* the new method to the *operators.*
3) Get final approval of all concerned on Safety, Quality, Quantity, and Cost.
4) Put the new method to work. Use it until a *better* way is developed.
5) Give *credit* where credit is due.

   The boss must be "sold" to get his approval for a trial run.

The operator may need to know more about it to give the new method a fair test.

The new method can yield increased production only after it's actually working.

Remember, today's best way, is only for today. Tomorrow there will be a better way—and you will work it out!

Stealing an idea is really a form of sabotage. Be open–minded to suggestions, even if many of them are "wild ideas." A really good one will come along that can contribute to victory.

Often a new method will "pop" into your mind without working through these FOUR STEPS. This is to be expected at the start. However, these "flashes" will soon be exhausted. Don't expect them to continue. For consistent improvement, you must think your way carefully through ALL of the FOUR STEPS. You will have to dig beneath the surface for most of your improvements.

MAKE THE JOB EASIER AND SAFER.

Remember, your purpose is to make jobs *easier* and *safer*—**NOT** to make people work harder or faster. This is NOT a speed up plan. It IS to show people how to work more effectively. Keep this basic purpose clearly in mind and you can't fail. Furthermore, you will find "improving job methods" is an interesting undertaking. Most important of all, you will contribute to *victory!*

HOW TO PREPARE INSTRUCTORS TO GIVE INTENSIVE JOB INSTRUCTION

07

Many companies have found it possible to organize effectively the training of new employees and experienced production workers in new skills so that the learning time is spent on the job on production work under actual shop conditions. On–the–job instruction is given by foremen, lead men, or, where large numbers of men need to be trained at one time, by special instructors.

Some companies have set up training sections separate from the regular production shop, using the output of such sections in the regular manufacturing process. Whether the instruction is given in production shops or in separate training sections, it is necessary to equip those selected to do the instructing with an organized knowledge of production operations and the ability to impart it to others.

In this bulletin are recommended the essentials for the preparation of instructors. It recognizes that modifications must be made to meet varying needs in different situations.

C. R. Dooley, Director
Training Within Industry

MAKING INSTRUCTORS

"*Instructor*" is used here to mean foreman, lead man or workman who has a major or full-time responsibility for breaking in production workers to new jobs.

Individual plant requirements in respect to the number of instructors, time available for training and degree of teaching skill necessary on specific jobs, will naturally vary. Job training covers a wide range, from an hour or two required to "break in" an employee on a simple, repetitive job to months for more difficult and complicated skills. There are four phases or steps usually followed in developing instructors:

1) Selection of those to be trained.
2) Arrangements for their training.
3) Content of the training program.
4) Supervision and follow–through.

1. SELECTION OF EMPLOYEES FOR TRAINING AS INSTRUCTORS

This is the most important step in the process since the ultimate success in training production workers depends upon the ability and skill of the job instructors. The following are important considerations in the selection of employees for training as instructors:

Personal aptitude should be given equal weight with job skill. It is common knowledge that good mechanics do not necessarily make good teachers. A genuine liking for working with people and an ability to express themselves clearly, patience and ability to get along with different kinds of people are important.

Recognized skill in the job to be taught. The degree of instructing skill required on any given job is governed to a large extent by the simplicity or complexity of the job.

A willingness to accept this kind of responsibility.

Some companies have used general intelligence, teaching aptitude and personality tests as aids in the selection of candidates for training.

2. ARRANGEMENTS FOR TRAINING INSTRUCTIONS

There are two sources through which trained instructors may be developed.

Under company auspices. If there is not already a supervisor of training within the company, one or more supervisors should be selected and trained to take up this responsibility. An outstanding foreman, engineer or junior executive might prove to be a good man for this work after he has had some practice. Visits to plants where such instruction is being carried on and help by a training specialist from another company would be useful in launching a program. Some State Universities and State Vocational Education Departments are manned to give assistance in training a supervisor to carry on this kind of work.

Usually it is desirable to release from other duties those selected to devote full time to the training of instructors, although in some companies the responsibility is taken over in addition to other duties. Elements of time, convenience, and number of instructors to be trained will be controlling factors.

By outside agencies. Some State Departments of Vocational Training offer courses in how to instruct on the job and are prepared to conduct classes for job instructors within a specific plant, or to hold classes for men from several plants at specially agreed upon central locations.

It has been found that the training of job instructors can best be done in groups of 8 to 10. Suitable quarters, away from the job should be arranged. Most companies have found it desirable to release men from all job responsibilities during the training, permitting them to give full–time intensive, attention to learning how to instruct.

3. CONTENT OF TRAINING PROGRAM

The scope of the training given and length of the training period will vary.

For example, the machine operator who will break in new workers on his kind of machine may require only 12 to 16 hours of training on how to instruct. The training in this instance would embrace the fundamentals of analyzing the one job he is to teach and supervised practice in how to quickly cover the key points of each operation with a new worker.

On the other hand, the full time instructor, who is responsible for the instruction of a number of new workers on several jobs requires a greater degree of teaching skill which may take 30 to 48 clock hours for him to acquire.

A typical program of instructor training, containing the major principles, is outlined below. It will not always be possible or even desirable to apply this entire pattern to all situations.

A) Job analysis for instruction purposes
The purpose here is to develop:

Ability on the part of the prospective instructor to make an analysis of the job to be taught. The experienced man often overlooks details of the job, which, because of his intimate knowledge, have become "second nature" to him. He must look carefully at every detail of a job from the beginner's viewpoint before attempting to teach it.

Ability to recognize and pull out the key operating points or "tricks of the trade" which are most vital to the successful performance of each operation.

Judgment as to the degree of detail to which it is necessary to go in breaking down a job, depending on the complexity of the operation to be taught and the knowledge the learner brings to the job.

These objectives can best be reached by requiring each member of the training group to analyze one job he will teach, under the guidance of the leader. This is done both in the conference group and individually with each trainee who makes an analysis of a job with which he is familiar out in the shop. A general discussion and comparison of analyses is then held with the group to bring about a common understanding of the technique.

Most of such analyses include all or part of the following:

Notes of the steps or operations necessary to do the job;
special words used in talking about the work, the product,
the tools, or doing the job;
Special precautions to insure required quality: ("getting it
done right the first time")
Notes on waste prevention, either of tools or materials;
safety and health precautions necessary for the learner to know in doing
the job;
Notes on the troublesome points where the learner must
exercise his own judgment;
Supplementary information such as how the product is used, and how
his part ties into other operations.

B) Planning the instruction
Each prospective instructor is required to make notes of a simple plan for putting over instruction which he is going to give. One or more of these units is tried out in a practice teaching situation (see below) and each demonstration is followed by review and discussion. Using the job analysis as a base, decision must be reached regarding:
What fundamentals must be driven home.
In what order the operations can best be taught.
What must be done to build up satisfactory output
after operations have been learned.
What facts must be given to the learner about the
job and when.

C) Teaching the job
The new instructor must be helped to understand the teaching process. The conference leader puts on sample demonstrations, involving real teaching situations to make clear each of the three following major requirements. The

group analyzes and discusses what the leader has done.

1) The steps through which the instructor leads a learner.

   In the process of teaching any part of a job, the new worker is only conscious of acquiring new knowledge and skill and is not aware of the four steps through which the instructor carries him:

   First, the learner's attention and interest is secured;

   Second, the learner is shown how to do that part of the job;

   Third, the instructor lets the learner try to do it, correcting mistakes before they become fixed in ineffective work habits;

   Fourth, the learner is put on his responsibilities but is closely watched by the instructor until he has gained skill and speed and confidence.

2) How the instructor puts across to the learner the ideas he must know to perform each operation.

3) How the instructor checks to see that the learner understands clearly.

D) The beginner's learning difficulties

It is necessary for the instructor to identify some of the learning difficulties inherent in jobs, how they may be classified, and their effect on the new worker in making it hard or easy for him to become proficient. There are at least six kinds of these learning difficulties:

Confusion over complex details.

Understanding the main idea.

"Unlearning" old habits.

Catching the "knack".

Getting the "feel".

Developing speed, ease and confidence.

Prospective instructors are placed in the position of "green" learners. The conference leader gives several teaching demonstrations, using simple units of instruction of real interest and new to the learner. Group discussion follows each demonstration to help the new instructor to get the "green" employee's point of view.

E) Practice teaching

Each new instructor must be given the opportunity to gain confidence that he can apply out in the shop what he is learning. Nothing is more helpful than practice under constructive coaching. Let him demonstrate how well he can apply the principles of job instruction in a practical teaching situation.

Throughout the entire period of training and as often as possible, each prospective instructor is required to teach a worker new to the company and to the job, one or more complete operations under the observation of the group and the leader. The operations to be taught are selected by the prospective instructor and are actual jobs which are a part of his own shop work. They are of such a nature that the complete operation can be covered with the learner in 20 to 25 minutes. How to use a file correctly, how to read a micrometer, how to perform a simple assembly operation, are examples of the type of instruction units used. The learners are usually sufficiently "green" to make it possible for their interest in learning something new to be genuine.

After each demonstration, through group discussion, the work of each prospective instructor is constructively criticized and evaluated.

4. SUPERVISION AND FOLLOW-THROUGH ON THE JOB

It is not sufficient to turn out a corps of trained instructors. The training of individual workers begins only at this point and there are several steps that may be taken to insure the instructor's effectiveness in getting workers into production quickly.

a) Provision should be made for a proper wage differential between the rate for instructors and the top rate of the work classification for which they are training workers. This policy provides an incentive to experienced men to attain competence in instructing new workers.

b) Special instructors, skilled men trained as instructors or trained lead men can safely handle five to ten men on production work. A check sheet or record of the workers performance, the speed with which the worker builds up skill, his method of doing the operations, rejects and spoilage and injuries are points to be closely checked on the job by the supervisor of training as well as by production supervisors.

In most companies, special instructors report administratively to the foreman responsible for production and are a part of the regular production force, but are under the technical direction of the staff training supervisor.

c) Frequent visits to the shop where the new instructor is working should be made by the training supervisor.

d) After instructors have been on the job for a month or two, they should be brought back for a half day conference in which instruction techniques are reviewed in the light of actual teaching experience. Periodic conferences of this type will help the instructor to improve his effectiveness.

e) Periodic reports regarding the success of new workers thus trained should be made to upper management. Having authorized the program, executives naturally are interested in its progress and success.

Unless the program results in a saving of *at least one half the time* usually taken by the old haphazard watching, telling, or just "showing 'em how" methods of breaking in new workers, the instructor training program has not been well planned or carried out.

HOW TO SELECT NEW SUPERVISORS

0 8

Every plant is always on the lookout for more supervisors. And, in rapidly expanding plants, the need for supervisors constantly becomes more acute. Good supervisors *are* hard to find. YOU HAVE TO TRAIN THEM.

Management is dependent on supervisors in order to reach the big group of workers in the plant, but not every worker wants to be a supervisor. Some actually refuse to take the responsibility. They do not want to give orders to their friends. Many are incapable of becoming good supervisors even though they would jump at the chance. They cannot plan, or follow through, or adjust their thinking to supervisory problems. Some people just can't quit "doing" and begin to direct *others* "to do." Poor judgment, slowness, indecisiveness, inflexibility, or annoying mannerisms prevent them from ever becoming effective supervisors.

Where, then, do we find men and women to train as supervisors? They must be *discovered* among the ambitious workers who are willing to pay the price of leadership, and who can work well with their associates. You spot them in the rank–and–file of *your own plant.*

Many plants give careful attention to the selection of top supervision, but "just appoint" quite casually the first–line supervisors, the ones who really are in closest touch with the workers who get out production. First–line supervisors are particularly important because they make up the group from which higher supervisors are most often selected. The greater a supervisor's responsibility, the more costly are the mistakes if the man is not really fitted for supervisory work.

Management delegates much of its responsibility to supervisors; hence, initial selection is of prime importance. Selection of men and women for supervisory positions is a definite responsibility of management, but assistance can be gained and the selection procedure improved if the recommendations of present supervisors and, sometimes, of both the union and individual workers are enlisted.

To find one leader you must get the facts about a number of possible candidates. You must choose carefully, because a mistake is costly. Personal prejudices and favoritism must be avoided. You must find a potential supervisor and train him. And don't fail to give him a feeling of PERSONAL Satisfaction in his new job.

C. R. Dooley, Director
Training Within Industry

PICKING THE WORKER TO BE TRAINED AS A SUPERVISOR

In slow moving times, supervisors often were created overnight by someone who said, "Tomorrow you take over the department. Now you are a foreman." Many of them turned out to be excellent. In easy–going times, the boss does know his men. But when five, twenty, or a hundred new supervisors are needed over a relatively short period in a rapidly expanding organization, there is little time to get well enough acquainted with workers to pass judgment on their qualifications for supervisory jobs. Under present conditions superintendents, and other company executives, don't know individual workmen well enough to take such "shots in the dark."

A more systematic method is needed. Selection is improved when the method includes participation by the present supervisors in the nomination of candidates; use of a uniform, objective measure of ability; and group judgment of candidates.

The selection program described in this bulletin has been outlined from industrial experience. It will help to spot the men and women who will be likely candidates for supervisory responsibility. The procedure is simple. And, it works.

EXPLAINING THE SELECTION PROGRAM TO MANAGEMENT

This selection program must be completely understood by top management and it must have management approval. Management must see that the approach is outlined to the operating heads. Responsibility for this selection program must be assigned to one operating or personnel man who will see that it is carried through all stages of operation.

Basically, there are six steps.

1) Present supervisors are asked to nominate candidates for additional supervisory jobs. It may also be feasible to ask for nominations from the workers and from union representatives.

2) Each supervisor's nominations are discussed with him.

3) A committee made up of an operating man, a personnel man, and another representative designated by management considers the records in order to prepare a list of candidates. Each candidate on this list is interviewed if he is not known to the members of the committee.

4) A standard objective measure, such as a test, is used to get information about the ability of each candidate.

5) The selection committee reviews all the qualifications of the candidates.

6) Those judged to be qualified for supervisory training are selected. This will provide, in addition to immediate needs, a reserve to meet future demands.

At the time that management decides to undertake this selection program and assigns the responsibility for operating it, a follow–up procedure to make sure it is carried out must be agreed upon. Follow–up responsibility must be assigned to a specific person.

1. STARTING THE SELECTION PROGRAM

The need must be explained to the present supervisors. They must be assured that their own jobs will not be unfavorably affected, and their cooperation must be won. To accomplish this it is necessary that an operating official who carries weight with the men call the supervisors together and inform them about the new method. He will need to:

a) Explain the *need* of having new supervisors coming along.

b) Raise the question, "Do we have workmen in the ranks who might be good supervisors, if properly trained?"

c) Emphasize that there is no thought of displacing present supervisors. It is *part of their jobs* to be on lookout for new talent. We can't afford to overlook good material. "All of us need understudies. You cannot move up until there is someone to take your place."

d) Make assignment: "Consider all the men in *your* departments. Don't talk to them about this topic, but think about them. Jot down names of all the men who you feel might have supervisory abilities. Do not suggest men from other departments—we want information about the men you really *know* something about from intimate working relationships. You know which men take the lead, and whether the others in the group accept this or resent it. You know, too, which ones learn new jobs most quickly."

e) Discuss personal qualities which are required of supervisors. Think in terms of the whole plant and what is expected of a supervisor.

f) Remind them that, while the supervisor has to know the work, the best operator is not necessarily the best supervisor, but he must have enough operating ability to merit respect from the workers he supervises.

g) Set a specific time to have list of names handed in.

Sometimes supervisors consciously or unconsciously stand in a man's way— if he is a good operator the supervisor does not want to lose him. Requiring each supervisor to name "two or three" will shake good men loose.

If management wishes to get nominations from the union and from individual workmen, the same steps of explanation should be followed.

2. GETTING INFORMATION ABOUT SUPERVISORY CANDIDATES

Not all the men and women who are suggested will be good possibilities. It is necessary to get more facts about those nominated. The supervisors who suggest names will be able to furnish much unrecorded detail.

The person assigned to head the selection committee will need to discuss with each supervisor the persons whose names he has suggested. Ask him to tell you why he nominated the person, but don't put him on the spot. This is a confidential fact–finding process, not a debate. Consider the following:

a) What is the man's work record, including accident record and absenteeism, as well as quality and quantity of production turned out? Does he *know* the work?

b) How does he get along with other workmen on the job?

c) Has he demonstrated such supervisory traits as ability to break in new men or to get men to cooperate with him on jobs? Do men go to him for help?

d) How does he conduct himself on the job?

e) Does he take the lead outside the plant—does he organize community events or sports?

f) Does he have ideas? Make constructive suggestions for improvements?

g) Has he been included in any training programs? How did he get along?

Some names may be withdrawn by the supervisors at this stage, and these persons need not know that they have been considered and judged unsuitable.

3. ROUGH SCREENING

Get personnel records (including health and safety records) for all men still on list, in order to have them considered by the selection committee. This committee should be made up of an operating executive, a personnel man, and another representative designated by management. One of these will be the man responsible for running the selection program. (This selection committee will be most effective if it has occasional "new blood.")

a) Search the records. Look for controlling factors, but do not give weight to "stale boners" that should have been forgotten long ago.

b) Retain the names of all those who look promising.

c) Consider the supervisor who made the nomination—can you go along with his opinion?

When these records are scrutinized, some additional workers will be considered unsuitable for supervisory development. These need not know that they have been rejected unless such information is considered advisable for personal development.

The surviving candidates who are not known to the members of the selection committee will be interviewed briefly to find out if possible about recent instances in which they have taken the lead.

4. GETTING INFORMATION FROM SUPERVISORY CANDIDATES

Judgment so far has been largely based on opinion, and there may be little uniformity in the records that are available for consideration. Selection is improved if the method includes the use of a standard, objective measure such as a test.

Some plants will already have records resulting from a recent test which has been used for all employees. In other plants production reports by workers may give a measure of ability to handle figures and fellow written instructions. In others it may be suitable to call the selected group of candidates together and give them a simple test to order to have a standard measure for all. There are many simple tests available commercially. Some companies prefer to draw up their own tests, using real problems from the plant. Twenty questions of the following type will make up a useful test:

If a rigger's hourly rate is 90 cents, what will it be if it is increased 10 percent?

What is the cost of a square foot of copper if a piece $1^{1/2}$ feet by $1^{1/2}$ feet costs 45 cents?

A bin holds 200 cubic feet of lime. If the bin is 10 feet long and 5 feet wide, how deep is it?

Divide 144 hours equally among three shifts.

If time and a half is paid for all time over 8 hours, how much will a man get for working 11 hours if his hourly rate is 60 cents?

A warehouse is four stories high, and the interior measurements are 50 by 200 feet. How many square feet of floor space?

How much more interest do you get in a year on $200 at 4% than on $200 at $3^{1/2}$ percent?

Divide: 45.3 / 921.402

If a wire 20 inches long is to be cut so that one piece is 2/3 as long as the other piece, how many inches long will the shorter piece be?

How much cheaper per pound is sugar at 12 pounds for a dollar than at 9 cents a pound?

When a plant draws up its own test forms, it usually is desirable to change the figures in the test with successive groups of candidates. Most commercial tests have alternate forms for repeated use.

Whatever test form is used, it is important to remember that the score is only one of the pieces of recorded information on which a decision is based,

Do not set a minimum or "passing" score—tests are used only to indicate those in the group who have the most ability to do simple figuring and to understand written directions. No time limit should be set—each person should be allowed to complete the form.

All candidates who are to be tested should be called together to hear about the selection program direct from management, rather than through rumors.

An operating executive, who has prestige with workers, explains the purpose:

48

a) Company is looking to the future.

b) More supervisors are needed.

c) Somebody has thought that each man in the room might make a good supervisor.

d) Supervisors have "headaches" but there are also rewards.

e) Not every man in the room will be a supervisor.

f) We need more facts. A practical test will be used to supplement the other records. It will help to indicate those who may became supervisors, but it is *not* going to be the *only* point on which the decision is made.

g) Even if you aren't selected, this isn't going to hurt you. *A man doesn't win every race he enters.*

There may be some who will indicate at this time that they are not interested in being considered for supervisory positions. If they wish, they should be allowed to leave before the test is given.

After the tests are scored they should be added to the records concerning the persons. Tests should **not** be returned. A score may be given to an individual if requested, but not until after the decision as to supervisory appointment has been made.

5. REVIEW OF ALL CANDIDATES' QUALIFICATIONS

The selection committee will now review each man's record separately:
  1) personal history data
  2) test record or other uniform measure
  3) other records that indicate the caliber of the man

When the committee considers this final assembly of records, it will be important to consider particularly the man's work history. Has the man had the kind of experience needed on the new assignment, or can he get it quickly? Remember that a man may make a good supervisor on one kind of work but not another. Consider present and prospective supervisory openings.

The selection committee should look for these qualities and abilities and the knowledge considered essential in *your* organization. In general, the best prospects are the men who:

a) have appropriate experience

b) are level–headed, intelligent, trainable, and willing to learn

c) have the personal characteristics you want of supervisors in your plant

d) have demonstrated their ability to get teamwork

e) are acceptable to their associates and present supervisors

f) are willing to take the responsibility of supervising

g) handle their personal affairs intelligently

h) can adapt themselves to change

Men who fail in one or more of those qualifications are doubtful prospects.

6. SELECTING THE PEOPLE FOR TRAINING

The selection committee now has the facts on which to base it decisions.

a) Accept or reject each man on list as a prospect for supervisory training. Decision should, if possible, be unanimous.

b) If a sufficient number of likely prospects are "voted in" at this stage, the doubtful cases can be held for future consideration.

c) If there is disagreement, so that no one gets unanimous endorsement, then further consideration should be given to nominees where there is majority approval of their qualifications.

d) If possible, observe the man breaking–in a new worker on the job, before final choice.

e) Let each candidate know where he stands.

This method of picking men indicates who will profit most from sound supervisory training. The next steps are to place him proper and see that he gets good training. Don't just allow him to pick up information as to the supervisor's job in a haphazard manner. Remember that you do *not* have a ready–made supervisor.

Some of the men may be appointed supervisors at once and get their training on the job. Others may be put in pre–supervisory training courses. Still others will be held as a reserve or pool. And there will be some who you know *never* will be appointed at all. All these candidates must be told *just where they stand.*

The "supervisory pool" must not be built up beyond the number needed within a reasonable time, such as three to six months. If there is not any turnover in the pool, the whole selection plan may be unpopular.

In order to follow the supervisory pool principle, it is necessary that:

a) management have some idea or estimate of the number of supervisors needed over some such period as three months

b) all promotions to supervisory positions come from the pool

WILL THIS WORK IN YOUR PLANT?

If your plant has an extensive employment procedure, you may already have recent test records that give you an objective, uniform measure—you may already have the information needed for Step 4.

If you do not have many supervisory positions to fill, it probably will be best not to set up a "pool" for if there are no appointments made from it in a reasonable length of time, the men will be more dissatisfied than if they had been told that someone else got the job and no more are open.

But, in any plant, it will pay to anticipate needs and go about supervisory selection in an organized manner rather than to look at it as "getting a man for the new shift tonight." And for any opening, it will pay to look at the qualifications of more than one man.

GAINS THROUGH GOOD SELECTION

Planning and foresight will pay dividends. The whole purpose of this method of picking men to be trained as supervisors is to identify the steps that will inventory the abilities of workers, so that "hidden talent" is not overlooked. A mans appearance and manner may not be impressive, yet he may have excellent supervisory ability.

No one person in the plant can possibly have all of the essential facts necessary to make "spot" decisions regarding the potential abilities of a man. Two or three men, familiar with the problem and acquainted with the men available for promotion, can do a better job of selecting than one can alone. The judgment of one supplements the others.

A review of the record and a discussion of the needs and facts *prevent* hasty decisions. Men with supervisory ability can be found among rank–and–file workers. That is the major source of supply. The men who will make good supervisors are there. This method gives you a simple way to *turn the searchlight* on the group and to find them.

IMPROVING SUPERVISORS' KNOWLEDGE OF WORK

09

There is no substitute for a thorough knowledge of the *very* work that the supervisor directs. The technical nature of the work is constantly changing, as products and processes change. Naturally, work that goes by the same name differs from company to company. It differs between departments.

Everyone admits that a supervisor in a rolling mill must know the steel business, but that is not enough—he has to know it as it applies to *his own plant*, in *his own* department. A supervisor in a coal mine must know coal mining, and he has to know his own plant's problems and methods of coal mining. A supervisor in an accounting department must know his organization's accounting practice, not just standard accounting practice found in text books. It is squarely up to each plant management to see that its own supervisors have this specific knowledge of *their* work. Naturally the same holds true for every business and every department, covering every feature of technical or operating work throughout the nation.

Many companies have had thoroughly capable supervisors fail because they lacked the proper knowledge of their work. This need not be. All that is necessary in a given plant is for *someone* to have a *plan* and see that it is followed.

That "someone" in each company is the manager, or some other person to whom management delegates this responsibility. Following are a few suggestions as to "plan." Naturally, each company should develop its own plan according to its own problems and the needs of its own supervisors.

C. R. Dooley, Director
Training Within Industry Service

WHERE PLANNING IS NEEDED

Here are a few of the more common circumstances which point to supervisors who need to know more about their work:

1) NEW SUPERVISORS

Many new supervisors are being appointed to replace men who go in the army or who are transferred or retired. Perhaps the new supervisors know all the operations and have the required technical background, or perhaps they don't. Sometimes the new supervisor is familiar only with those operations on which he worked. Likely he has only passing familiarity with the much larger group of operations for which he is now responsible.

2) EXPERIENCED SUPERVISORS ON NEW JOBS

Many times "old hands" are placed on new jobs in new or converted plants or in different departments. Often it is assumed that years of service alone mean adequate technical knowledge even though the experience is limited to one or two operations.

3) CHANGED JOBS

Countless thousands of jobs have changed because of the necessity of making new products out of new materials on new equipment. Usually the newer the product or materials or equipment, the less certain and less standard the operations. Often these are the very jobs that change again and again, as perhaps metallurgical changes in the materials are developed and as new operating procedures are found necessary.

54

SOME WAYS OF GIVING SUPERVISORS KNOWLEDGE OF THE WORK

1) INSTRUCTION FROM SUPERIOR

If, for example, a foreman is newly promoted to his job, sometimes the general foreman can, over a period of time, give him a thorough knowledge of the work. This is the ideal arrangement, for everyone does and should look to his boss for guidance and direction in just about everything connected with his job.

Often, however, instruction from a superior takes the form of guidance on day–to–day procedures only. The superior may not have the time—or may think he hasn't—to instruct the new supervisor in many details. Hence, leaving the training job solely up to every superior isn't an assurance that it will be done. How much the "boss" can do—(or *will* do!)—should be carefully considered. However, it is sometimes surprising how much "the boss" can help when he is *required* to do so by the "big boss."

2) INSTRUCTION BY OUTSIDE SPECIALISTS

Outside specialists can help to a marked degree. A common example of such is the help provided by most machinery and equipment companies. Most of these companies will arrange for one of their representatives to come to the plant when the equipment is new and stay for a period ranging from a few days to several weeks. Full advantage should be taken of all such offers.

In other cases a specialist from the ordnance department or from the original contractor company will spend time with a supervisor on the job. Specialists from laboratories or observers from the field of battle provide two more kinds of help. Every company can readily assemble the list of such outside specialists who might be used.

The training itself should be done right on the job. There is no better method than having a specialist spend a great deal of time right in the shop discussing with the supervisor the detailed problems of the job.

3) PLANNED WORK EXPERIENCE

Often a supervisor—new or experienced—may need to be instructed in performing several manual jobs in order that he can direct them well. This instruction is to give him familiarity with the operations themselves. Of course, there is much more to know about a job than the details of mechanical operation. But where these skills should be learned, there is no substitute for "learning them by doing them."

Many a supervisor feels he is "stepping down" when he runs a machine for a few days or a few weeks. He feels he has lost his status in the eyes of his workers because the workers can perform the operations better than the boss.

Any supervisor who wants to succeed, however, must accept this risk. Actually he runs no risk at all if he is the "right kind of a guy". Workers admire the boss who is willing to "get his hands dirty" in order to "know what he is talking about." Doing this very thing has "made" many a successful supervisor.

4) EXPERIENCE IN ANOTHER PLANT

Sometimes a supervisor can be sent to another plant for a short time to pick up some technical knowledge or operating procedures. Thousands of plants have cooperated with each other on this basis already. Even peace–time competitors in many cases have helped "make a man" for each other in war–time.

5) JOB BREAKDOWNS

A sure–fire way of getting thoroughly informed as to operations or procedures is to have supervisors make an accurate, written outline of each operation or process. No particular form of breakdown is necessary. However, any supervisor who has used either the Job Instruction or Job Methods form of breakdown would certainly understand thoroughly those operations he "broke down."

Much time and money has been wasted by supervisors who just observed and talked about a manufacturing process and "thought they knew" all about it. Companies have been known to send supervisors to observe the same process four or five times before they caught all the operating details. If these same supervisors had been required to make a complete breakdown of the process, they would have caught all the details and tricks of the trade the first time.

Making breakdowns at first may appear to be something of a task. However, they became easier to make with practice. Their use saves so much time, effort and costly mistakes that the making of them is justified a hundred times over.

6) MANUALS

The use of manuals is common, and they have many values. Manuals are available from a variety of sources, or maybe written in the plant. However, not even the most complete manual should ever be regarded as the sole answer to a supervisor's need for technical and operating information.

7) HELP FROM ENGINEERS

Help from one or more of the company's engineering groups is often the most valuable that a supervisor can receive. Some engineers take a "high–brow" attitude toward the "poor shop man." On the other hand, some shop supervisors consider themselves the only "practical" men. They look down on the engineers. Getting the two groups close together will produce outstanding results.

Engineers can help in several ways. The best way of all is for an engineer to spend time in the shop *with* the operating supervisor right on the job. An engineer can also hold a series of meetings with plant supervisors where he presents technical knowledge or answers questions.

Getting appropriate understanding that the engineers are *expected* to help plant supervisors is essential. Top management must see to this. Engineers will find that this is not a "one may" process. They too, get extremely valuable help from shop supervisors.

8) PLANT CONFERENCES

In some companies there are regular staff meetings to pass along information at each executive and supervisory level. In other companies these are occasional. In still others there are special meetings about company products and manufacturing methods. The question of "how many meetings" is a vital one. The only answer is to hold as many meetings as are necessary to be sure that *every* supervisor knows *every* single thing that is necessary for him to know in order that he do a *top-grade* job.

9) SUPPLEMENTARY INSTRUCTION

Extremely valuable supplementary instruction may be received from the engineering colleges and universities as well as the vocational schools. If the plant is not near one of these institutions, very often an extension program can be especially arranged. If a company desires certain special courses to be developed, and the number of persons justifies such a course, these schools will often develop such special programs. This supplementary instruction is of value to the *plant* only if the program meets the supervisors' *specific* needs.

RESPONSIBILITY FOR DEVELOPING SUPERVISORS

Acquiring knowledge about supervisory work should not be left to the supervisor's initiative. There are those who argue that leaving it "up to each person" is one of the tests of initiative, one of the ways of showing who is worthy of promotion.

Unfortunately things do not always work out this way. Often the thoroughly able supervisor will not take the initiative; he may think of it, he may not know what he needs, he may not know what is available. Sometimes he feels that such action might be improper or that he would be regarded by his fellows as selfish and "forward." Conversely, a supervisor with limited abilities but with devastating ambition may voluntarily seek more information about the technical side of his work, be disappointed if he does not get recognition—and resent it.

Improving supervisors' technical knowledge should be planned just as carefully as any other company program. The management should let it be known that every supervisor is *expected* to keep abreast of the technical demands of his job and that a *plan* is to be followed in accomplishing this end. Someone in the company should be designated to counsel with each executive and supervisor concerning the needs of each of his subordinates. He should also help each executive and supervisor plan for the development of each subordinate. In larger companies this person is usually the training director. In smaller companies it is often a production executive who gives part of his time to this work.

The procedure between the training director and a line executive is simple. Together they set down what a subordinate *now* knows about the job. Then they set down what he *needs* to know. Next they decide which of the above suggestions—or others—should be used. The line executive is then ready to call in the subordinate, go over the plan with him, and see that the subordinate gets the required knowledge.

KEEPING SUPERVISORS INFORMED ABOUT THEIR RESPONSIBILITIES

10

This bulletin outlines a simple plan for giving training to supervisors in the knowledge of their responsibilities. It is prepared especially for those managers who have the point of view of "anticipation and prevention" rather than "discovery and correction." It is for those who look beneath the surface for the solution of their supervisory problems.

It is important that every supervisor know not only the technical phases of his job but also just what his responsibilities are. Since these responsibilities change, it is necessary that the plan for keeping supervisors informed of their responsibilities shall operate continuously.

No plant management can hold a supervisor responsible for things about which he has not been informed. This plan is only an outline for a method of approach within which any company can develop its own program in detail according to its own problems and needs.

C. R. Dooley, Director
Training Within Industry

RESPONSIBILITY FOR DEVELOPING SUPERVISORS

The one dominant influence in each supervisor's life, just as in the case of each employee, is his boss. Therefore, the best supervisory training in the world is having a "good boss." The most successful supervisory development program is one sponsored and directed by top management.

This plan enables each officer and supervisor to keep his subordinate supervisors informed in an organized manner. Without some organized plan this job is easily crowded out of the picture by the rush and pressure of production duties, and the supervisor acquires information about his responsibilities in a haphazard manner through costly experience.

It is essential that the program start at the top, the president or at least the general manager of a given plant.

BASIC FEATURES OF THE PLAN

1) Acceptance by top management of the responsibility for adequately informing supervisors of their responsibilities.

2) Regular conferences at each organizational level, sponsored and directed by line organization supervisors.

3) Frank discussion, free consultation, and appropriate action concerning company policies and individual responsibilities, at each level.

4) The appointment of staff training men to direct the routine of these meetings, see that arrangements are made, notices sent out, agenda prepared, and reports issued.

SETTING UP THE PROGRAM

The initial meeting should be called by the chief officer of the company or plant and attended by his immediate staff and other key people who are regularly associated with them.

The object of this meeting is to discuss the need for keeping supervisors informed about their responsibilities and the details of a proposed program for accomplishing this objective. The head of the company or plant should be the active chairman of the meeting. A training man should assist the head of the company or plant in laying out the agenda for the meeting and should attend the meeting to lend assistance in planning the later program.

Naturally there are certain problems outside the ability of the supervisor to do anything about, but practically every company problem—plant extension, equipment, finance, quality control, shipping schedules, costs, labor relations, etc., should be touched upon to determine at the very outset the scope of the responsibilities to be carried at each successive layer of supervision. Succeeding conferences on lower levels should each determine definitely just what responsibilities are to be carried by each supervisor on each level of supervision.

The extent to which it appears that information about responsibilities is lacking on the various levels of supervision will determine the character of the program both as to agenda and as to schedule of meetings.

1)   PERIODIC CONFERENCES FOR SUPERVISORS ON ALL LEVELS

Each chief supervisor should meet regularly with those supervisors who report to him. Experience will determine the length and frequency of these meetings but usually one and one–half hours every two to four weeks will be found satisfactory. The best meetings are those for which the agenda is brief and the conference itself kept informal. The make–up of the conferences must be determined according to each company's organizational structure. The criterion is to have in each meeting only those supervisors who have comparable responsibilities.

As soon after the close of the first meeting as convenient, each member of that conference should call a conference of those supervisors reporting to him and carry on the discussion. This process should continue on down the organization until the first–line supervisors have been reached.

This pattern is of vital importance. It includes regularity of meetings, topics to be discussed, promptness of sending out reports, promptness of following up unfinished business, and many other items vital to steering the effectiveness of the program as a whole.

The head of each group should always be present unless unavoidably detained, and should never fall into the habit of leaving the conduct of the meeting to a substitute because of casual reasons. A conference which is not worthy of the attention of the supervisory chief is not worth holding at all.

2)   CONFERENCE LEADERSHIP

The executive or supervisor in charge of each group at each level must be chairman of his own conference. If he is a trained conference leader he may lead the meeting himself. If not, he may turn the leadership of the discussion over to a conference leader or he may open and close the meeting and tactfully participate in the discussion but depend upon the conference leader to keep the discussion on the topics and on schedule.

Some supervisors inexperienced in leading conferences will

quickly become familiar with the procedure and gradually take more detailed responsibility. Others will never attain competence in using the conference method, and still others may leave the conduct of the meeting to a conference leader just so they can participate in the discussions and otherwise aid the program as a member of the group. Whatever procedure is used, there must never be any doubt that the supervisor in charge is responsible for the conference and is personally going to see that it is a success—that everyone who attends feels it was worth his time.

3)   AGENDA OF CURRENT SUPERVISORY PROBLEMS

The responsibility for determining the agenda rests with the conference conducted by the top executive. The company training director, meeting with groups at all levels, maintains the thread of continuity and sees that action is not delayed and that proper reports are rendered. In some plants, particularly in large companies, there may be a full–time conference secretary.

The first step in planning a series of agenda is to find out what policies have already been set down in writing. This applies particularly to employment, training, hours, wages, transfers, promotions, seniority, layoff, discharges. Plans include insurance, hospitalization, sick benefits, vacations, savings, stock purchase, and incentives; procedures include methods of wage payment, routine for reporting accidents, and method of arranging transfers; rules, covering a wide field, are often not too sharply defined.

Quite often there is nothing in writing on a supervisor's responsibility as to scheduling, cost, maintenance, quality, waste, and interdepartmental relationships. Each supervisor should also have knowledge of legal restrictions and regulations which effect plant operations. There will be written material on union contracts and often on a grievance procedure.

Each conference, from the top down, places on its agenda two kinds of topics:
> Those which concern its own particular group only.
> Those which should be brought to the attention of
> other groups.

Many conclusions arrived at must be passed on to groups of *lower* levels for execution but many of the conclusions and some of the opinions should be passed up to groups on *higher* levels for their information. One of the major results of this program of conferences is to help break down the natural insulation between an executive and the entire structure below him.

Many suggestions and opinions, if tactfully presented, will be welcomed by the higher officers and supervisors of a plant or company.

4)   SUBJECT MATTER FOR SUPERVISORY CONFERENCES

The top conference group usually develops enough topics for discussion by groups at lower levels to keep the schedule over-crowded. The problem generally is how to eliminate topics for discussion rather than how to suggest them. Additional topics also flow upward.

However, for those who may not know how to get started, the following suggestions may be helpful:

Open the meeting by presenting one or two topics which have been handed down by the next higher group.

If the company has no written industrial relations policy, each group may develop initial drafts of such policies and present them to the higher groups.

If the company has well defined written industrial relations policies, each group may periodically review them in the light of current requirements and recommend changes to the higher groups.

Recent government rulings, labor agreements, and training programs, affecting responsibilities of supervisors may be discussed.

Questions of customer service, quality, maintenance, inspection, store–keeping, shipping, often involve misunderstanding as to just which supervisor is responsible for what.

The most effective method yet discovered by which areas of responsibility and authority can be clearly determined, over-lapping of functions eliminated, internal jealousies dissipated, and procedures clarified and simplified, is through *group analysis of the responsibilities of the individual departments, divisions, supervisors, and getting group agreement to conclusions.* Frequently such agreements clear up difficulties between departments of different levels. There is scarcely an activity that is not materially changed and improved when subjected to the group analysis of the various executives and supervisors affected.

All supervisors need up–to–date information concerning the company, its products, and its technical processes. This is easily accomplished by inviting company specialists to attend group meetings and lead discussions in their respective fields of activity.

63

5)   IMPORTANCE OF FIRST-LINE SUPERVISORS

Having general matters start with the chief executive group and flow down through the various conferences sometimes requires special help when such matters reach first–line supervisors. If there are two or three work shifts, it may be impossible for the foreman to meet with all his supervisors. Perhaps it is not possible to remove all supervisors from the floor at one time. In such cases the foreman or general foreman can delegate to a conference leader the responsibility of conducting some of the conferences for him.

It is important to remember that information tends to lose its clarity and significance as it passes from one level to another. A report from the first–line supervisors telling their understanding of the information should be asked for when there is any possibility of misunderstanding.

HOW TRAINING CAN BE DONE METHODS & AIDS

11

HOW TO CONDUCT A PLANT MEETING

Meetings are common in any plant—when two or more people get together, it's a meeting. One person—the person who wants to get something out of the meeting—needs to have a definite purpose for the meeting, needs to have planned what will be discussed, and needs to have ready any material required for the discussion.

Too few meetings are planned on that basis. Consequently, the meetings are meaningless, get no results, become unpopular, and may be attended only occasionally.

Meetings *can* serve a useful purpose—they can be the method of informing, or consulting, or training, or getting acceptance.

There are four steps in running a meeting:

1) GET READY
>Define objective clearly. List points to cover.
>Plan exhibits or aids. Find suitable place.
>Be sure everything is ready.

2) OPEN THE MEETING
>Start on time.
>State what you are trying to accomplish.
>Find out what is already known about the subject.

3) GUIDE THE DISCUSSION
>Question group and individuals.
>Get across ideas with reports, samples, etc.
>Discuss possible solutions.

4) CLOSE THE MEETING
>Make sure of common understanding about "next steps."
>Finish on time.
>All meetings, small or large, will be improved if they are systematically planned in this way.

1) GET READY

Define clearly just what you are trying to accomplish. If there is no objective, do not hold the meeting. Decide what materials—samples, models, charts, and reports—should be taken along, and get them ready. Find a suitable place for the meeting—a room that is large enough, where lighting and ventilation are adequate, where you will not be interrupted or disturbed by noises.

Set a time for the meeting—do not make it any longer than necessary. Consider the reason you are having the meeting. Is it worth the collective time that will be spent on it? Notify people who are to attend—give them time to arrange to come, but do not make the interval so long the meeting is forgotten. A very important meeting may make a personal, last–minute check of expected attendance worthwhile.

Before the time set for the meeting, check to see whether equipment is on hand. Plan timing of an intermission if the meeting is to last more than two hours.

2) OPEN THE MEETING

Start the meeting on time. If you habitually wait for stragglers, you penalize those who are prompt.

State clearly just what you are trying to accomplish. This is fundamental to concentrating attention on some specific item which you want understood, accepted, or opened up. Put your objective on the blackboard—refer to it, hold to it. Find out what members of the group already know about the subject—fill in gaps.

3) GUIDE THE DISCUSSION

Use a questioning technique. Direct questions to individuals, not to the group. Do not "call on" a member, or introduce the question by his name. Keep all the members following you by using a name at the end of the question. Avoid questions which can be answered by "yes" or "no." If some members are reluctant to participate, direct leading or obvious questions to them.

Don't let any one person monopolize the discussion. Be ready to break in with a thank you—and have a question for another member ready. If one member stands out alone, get other members of the group to answer his questions.

Find out whether anything interferes with accomplishing the objective—and what it is. Guide the discussion toward concrete evidence and specific factors you can do something about. Discuss possible solutions. List these interferences and solutions on the board. Talk while you do board work— and do not block the view of the whole board while you write. Summarize frequently.

Use models, samples, and other materials to illustrate ideas.

4) CLOSE THE MEETING

Keep the discussion on the subject of the discussion, and watch your schedule so you can close on time.

Make sure that there is a common understanding about "Who is going to do what, and when." Put this on the board—then put it on your list of work to do if the importance or complexity makes it advisable to give every member of the group a written report on action decided or policy accepted.

SELECT THE MOST EFFECTIVE AID

MOTION PICTURES

Use when overall view or impression is needed, when noise of actual operation would prevent explanation, when actual use or operation of product is at a distance, when operation has to be slowed down or stopped for explanation, when viewing operation would hamper production, when it is safer to get preliminary view from film.

FILM STRIPS OR SLIDES

Same as for films except motion is not required or desirable, or expense or lack of equipment prevents use of motion pictures.

PROJECTIONS

Where all of group needs to look at same drawing, chart or photograph simultaneously and leader wants to focus all attention on one specific point at a time.

ILLUSTRATIONS, CHARTS, DIAGRAMS

When process flow is important, when trends need to be emphasized, for comparative statistics.

SAMPLES

To show real object.

CUT–AWAYS

To show structure of opaque object, relative position.

MOCK–UPS

When finished assembly covers parts, when finished product is not available, when safety is involved.

LARGE SCALE MODELS

Large enough to permit handling, identify small parts.

SMALL SCALE MODELS

Permit operation without using large quantities of material, make a whole operation visible.

EXHIBITS

Show finished products, kinds of scrap, results of poor work, effect of breaking safety regulations.

BLACKBOARD

For sketches, diagrams, outlines, definitions, directions, summaries, assignments.

BOOKS, MANUALS, PAMPHLETS INSTRUCTION SHEETS

For standard information and guides, manufacturer's information, reference, background.

CARTOONS, POSTERS

To arouse interest, attract attention.

	Use It	Don't Use It
Demonstration	To show manipulative operation.	When note–taking is required.
	To clarify principles or theory	In place of practice.
	To show use of equipment	
Practice	To develop performance skill To help retain information	On a theoretical problem but only on a real one.
Discussion	To make people think To emphasize factual material To warm up or review To give reasons	To fill in time Without a good leader To present new material In place of practice
Conference Meetings	To get benefit of previous experience. To get opinions and help. To modify opinions. To develop understanding. To get acceptance.	Unless people are already in-formed about subject As initial training. In place of practice.
Lecture Meetings	When presenting informational Supplemented by visual aids.	For material with many details. For training in a skill

DEVELOPING ALL ROUND SKILLED CRAFTSMEN THROUGH APPRENTICESHIP

12

This bulletin embodies the principal features of apprenticeship taken from the best practices found in leading industries and will serve as a basis for apprentice training in practically all situations. It was prepared with the assistance of the staff of the Apprentice–Training Service, War Manpower Commission. The field and headquarters staff of Training Within Industry assists the Apprentice–Training Service by promoting the use of apprenticeship and advancing worker programs. On the other hand, many Apprentice–Training representatives are serving as Training Within Industry panel members.

The training of production workers in operations requiring a single skill is not a substitute for apprenticeship. Both programs have a distinct place in emergency war production and should be carried on simultaneously. Trade apprenticeship should be regarded not only as a long–term program from which industry must procure most of its future skilled craftsmen but also as a source from which set–up men, lead men, as well as some future supervisory and technical personnel may be drawn.

Apprentices trained under the standards of the Federal Committee earn their wages from the beginning, and they carry their weight in output.

C. R. Dooley, Director
Training Within Industry

APPRENTICESHIP POLICIES FOR WARTIME

Apprenticeship is a war activity and must continue to expand to meet war needs. Planning for a long war is necessary for victory, and apprenticeship is a long–range program. Its features are really expanded by the war program, for a certain number of all–round skilled workers will always be needed to supervise the large number of workers knowing only one skill or a small group of skills, and to perform that small proportion of highly skilled work which mass production cannot eliminate.

Skilled men are needed to produce delicate and complicated mechanisms for anti–aircraft guns, airplanes, and other vital war weapons. Since a large number of present skilled workers fall into the older age groups, apprentices must be trained both to replace these older workers and to meet the war demand for additional highly trained journeymen. Even while in training, apprentices frequently are assigned to the important function of breaking in new workers on single machines.

The Federal Committee on Apprenticeship recommends that apprenticeship programs be continued and maintained with new vigor, and that solutions be found for war time apprentice training problems which will serve the pressing needs of war production for all–round skilled workers and also serve the best interests of the nation's young people. For the war's duration the Federal Committee has made the following recommendation concerning the training and utilization of apprentices:

1) Establish apprenticeship programs on the basis of regular peace time standards, but including such wartime standards as are necessary to develop trained workers essential to the conduct of the war.

2) Amend existing apprenticeship programs to provide for the training of apprentices as rapidly as they can acquire reasonable proficiency in each trade process.

3) Improve job supervision and related classroom instruction of apprentices so that the period of learning time may be shortened. Advancements should be measured by objective tests established or given by joint apprenticeship committees.

4) Where it is imperative in the interests of war production to secure all-round skilled workers in the minimum of time, apprentices should be selected from groups least vulnerable to military service. Preferred groups in this category include married men from 20 to 30 years of age with one or more children; men classified as ineligible for military service for physical reasons; military personnel released from active service; and, for some trades, women.

5) Where the need is for all-round skilled men in the future, the Committee recommends that apprentices be selected from the 16 and 17 year age group but without the expectation that they will be deferred if the time comes when they are needed in the military service.

6) Because in some war production plants and industries, there are acute shortages of skilled workers to serve as supervisors, foremen, lead men, and job instructors, the Committee recommends that advanced apprentices be moved into any job classification which will permit utilization of their highest skills; and that they should be paid the wage rate applicable to the job to which they are promoted.

7) Where advanced apprentices exist in any plant in excess of the number of jobs available for the utilization of their highest skills, the Committee recommends that employers and employees voluntarily set up machinery for the reclassification of such advanced apprentices and for their transfer to other plants where there is a critical need for such skilled workers.

The needs of each industry and of each plant should be carefully analyzed and the apprentice training program should be worked out in the manner best suited to fill those needs.

APPRENTICESHIP PROGRAM

The objective of apprenticeship is the development of all-round skilled craftsmen. This is accomplished by a program of production work assignments in which each apprentice follows a pre-determined work training schedule which is accompanied by supplementary instruction. The major part of apprentice training is done on the job, at productive work.

A well-balanced program provides not only for efficient training in trade skills, but allows time enough for the apprentice to mature as a responsible worker.

On the other hand, the program should enable each apprentice to progress according to his individual learning ability. Some apprentices are thus able to successfully complete their training in a somewhat shorter time than the established period.

DEFINITION OF "APPRENTICE" AND MINIMUM STANDARDS OF APPRENTICESHIP

The Federal Committee on Apprenticeship has issued the following brief descriptions:

1) Definition of "Apprentice":

The term "apprentice" shall mean a person at least 16 years of age who is covered by a written agreement registered with a State Apprenticeship Council or the Federal Committee on Apprenticeship, providing for not less than 4,000 hours of reasonably continuous employment for such person, and for his participation in an approved schedule of work experience through employment, which is supplemented by 144 hours per year of related classroom instruction.

2) Basic Standards:

a) An apprentice–able occupation is considered one which requires 4,000 or more hours to learn.

b) A schedule of the work processes to be learned on the job.

c) A progressively increasing scale of wages for the apprentice should average approximately 50 per cent of the journeyman's rate over the period of apprenticeship.

d) Provision for related classroom instruction (144 hours per year of such instruction is normally considered necessary).

e) The terms and conditions of the employment and training of each apprentice to be stated in written agreement and registered with the State Apprenticeship Council.

f) Review of local apprenticeship programs by a State Apprenticeship Council.

g) Apprenticeship should be jointly established by the employer and the employees.

h) Adequate supervision and the keeping of records should be required for all Apprenticeship programs.

THE APPRENTICE–TRAINING SERVICE

The functions of the staff of the Apprentice–Training Service are:

1) to promote sound labor standards of apprenticeship in industry by joint cooperation between management and labor

2) to provide technical assistance in the establishment or improvement of apprenticeship systems

3) to assist in the development of programs for trainees at less than the apprenticeship level

4) to provide advice and assistance on labor problems affecting training

The actual training of apprentices is provided by industry under planned programs meeting the standards recommended by the Federal Committee. The Apprentice–Training Service, with the cooperation of State Apprenticeship Councils, promotes and assists industry in developing such training programs.

SETTING UP AN APPRENTICESHIP PROGRAM IN AN INDUSTRIAL PLANT

The responsibility for the apprentice program should be assigned to one person qualified to handle it. Most companies find that the plan is productive of best results when responsibility for it is placed upon a single supervisor fitted for this work by both personal qualities and experience. This is a full time job in large plants and a part–time job, but a major responsibility, in smaller plants.

Experience with well established apprenticeship plans indicates that, in setting up a program, action should be taken on the items indicated in the sections which follow. Experience in plants having bargaining agreements with organized labor shows that joint committees of management and labor can most effectively establish policies and procedures for the training of apprentices covering all following points:

1) Determine the skilled occupations in which apprentices are to be trained.
2) Determine the number of apprentices to be trained.
3) Establish the term of apprenticeship.
4) *Provide for instruction and coaching on the job*, including the selection and scheduling of work experience.
5) Arrange for classroom instruction in related trade subjects.
6) Establish a wage scale for apprentices in relation to the going rates for skilled workers in the trades in which apprentices are to be trained. The scale should be so established as to provide periodic increases as apprentices progress. *Apprentices produce while learning, and their wages should correspond to the level of their skills.*
7) Provide for periodic tests of the progress of apprentices.

SELECTING CANDIDATES FOR APPRENTICESHIP

The ultimate success of an apprenticeship plan depends more upon the ability and character of the young men selected than upon any other single factor in the program. The following are fundamental considerations in selecting those to be trained:

1. Give special attention to the character (including indications of perseverance), mechanical aptitude, and intelligence of candidates. Consider not only subjects (such as arithmetic and blueprint reading) which have been covered in school, but also whether school progress was at a normal rate or better.

2. Take full advantage of all information available in plant personnel records for those already employed who desire to be all–round skilled workers.

3. Consult with school authorities for additional evidence of aptitude and suitability of apprentice candidates.

4. Establish a definite probationary period to serve as double check on the suitability of those selected.

5. Usually there are candidates who have some trade experience who can be given credit on the term of apprenticeship and who will complete the program in less than the full period. This is particularly helpful in launching a new program and will make available some trained men at an earlier date.

CARRYING ON THE PROGRAM

Experience with well established programs indicates, that continuous attention is needed an the two basic features of apprentice training, i.e., shop experience and related instruction.

1) *Shop Experience*: It is essential that carefully organized instruction be given to each apprentice when he starts to work on each new job. In some larger plants where the number of apprentices justifies, a section of the regular shop is equipped and used especially for apprentices.

The Apprentice Shop is not a practice department. All work is productive and standards are uniform with other sections of the plant. The arrangement is desirable simply because a great deal of individual instruction and attention can be given when the apprentices are grouped. This contributes to thorough mastery, of the trade and to shortened learning time. It also enables the apprentice to do a good job alongside the journeymen Awe he goes into the regular department.

The Apprentice Shop is often used during second and third shifts as a convenient unit for training production specialists on particular machines.

In small plants the apprentice's shop experience is gained entirely on regular jobs in the shop. In either case care should be used in choosing the kind of production work, bearing in mind its teaching and experience value. The thoroughness and speed with which the apprentice learns his trade will largely depend upon the instruction ability and continuous coaching of the foremen and journeymen immediately over him.

In cooperation with foremen the apprentice supervisor, or the person in the small plant who is responsible for apprenticeship as part of his duties, should have authority to move apprentices from job to job in accordance with the planned training schedule. Apprentices should be given appropriate increases in their pay when justified by increased skill and knowledge, but according to the pre-determined schedule.

2) *Related Instruction:* Public vocational schools usually provide related instruction on technical subjects, although some companies establish their own plans. This supplemental instruction should coincide with current production experience. Ordinarily, up to ten percent of the working hours should be devoted to such related instruction.

COMMUNITY APPRENTICESHIP PROGRAM

Occasionally smaller plants or activities which cannot provide the breadth of on-the-job experience required for apprentice training will combine with other plants and activities in the community. By routing apprentices from jobs providing training in one set of skills in one company, to those which furnish experience in another set of skills in another company, the full range of training can be covered cooperatively.

THE ADVANCING WORKER PROGRAM

In order to meet needs for highly skilled men where there is not enough time to develop all-round craftsmen, the Apprentice-Training Service has set up its Advancing Worker program. This provides for training through a progressive series of jobs with supplementary instruction where needed. Well-rounded skill is attained in specific work of a type which is ordinarily part of a craft or trade.

COOPERATION IN APPRENTICESHIP PROGRAM

The Apprentice-Training Service operates throughout the United States largely through its regional offices. In addition, other public agencies and groups cooperate in the training of apprentices. State and federal employment bureaus assist in setting up the definite selection measures which are necessary, and vocational education funds and facilities supply much of the related instruction.

Sample Program for Tool and Die-Making Apprentices

Sequence of Work Assignments and proportion of Time Spent in Production Shop Work and Related Instruction

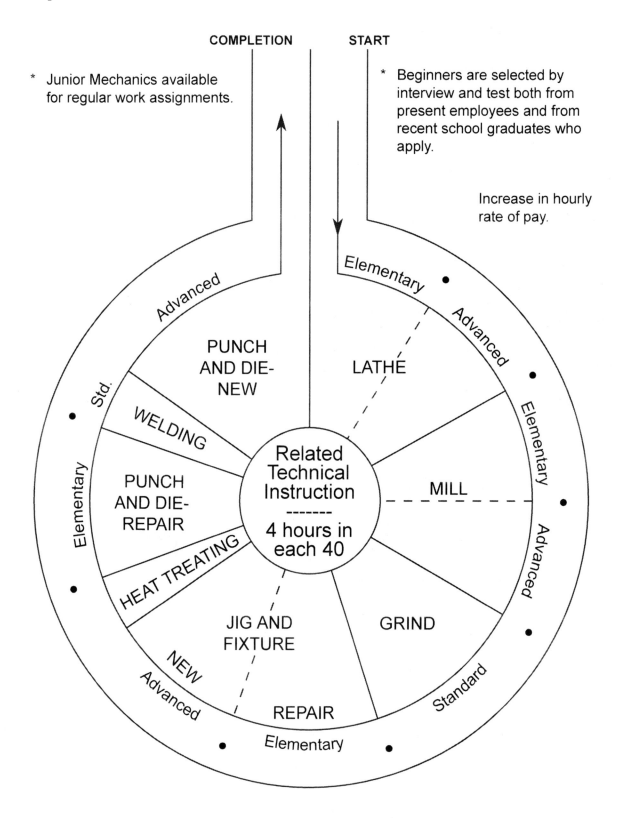

COMPLETION   **START**

* Junior Mechanics available for regular work assignments.

* Beginners are selected by interview and test both from present employees and from recent school graduates who apply.

Increase in hourly rate of pay.

Diagram labels (clockwise from START):
Elementary — LATHE — Advanced
Elementary — MILL — Advanced
Standard — GRIND
Standard
Elementary — REPAIR
Advanced — NEW — JIG AND FIXTURE
HEAT TREATING
PUNCH AND DIE-REPAIR
Elementary
Std. — WELDING
Advanced — PUNCH AND DIE-NEW

Center: Related Technical Instruction
----
4 hours in each 40

TYING IN PRE–EMPLOYMENT WITH ON–THE–JOB TRAINING

13

Training prior to employment helps shorten the time needed for developing skill on the job. With pre–employment instruction, the new employee learns the new job more quickly. He adjusts himself more readily to factory surroundings. He grasps sooner the language of the factory. And more important, he acquires beginning skill. Thus, a shorter break–in period is required before the new worker reaches good production standards.

Pre–employment training is most valuable when it is closely related to the job that the prospective worker will fill. When pointed toward a specific job, it has greater appeal and the student is more eager to learn. The result is better training.

This bulletin is based upon programs in successful operation. Experience shows that success depends upon a sound relationship between instruction under public auspices and training in the factory.

C. R. Dooley, Director
Training Within Industry

PURPOSE OF PRE-EMPLOYMENT TRAINING

The chief purpose of instruction in advance of employment in war production is to enable the worker to perform his tasks more effectively and reach production efficiency more rapidly when he goes on the job. The beginner becomes acquainted with the tools, machines and materials employed in the industry where he will work and acquires operational skills based upon routines and safeguards in common use.

NATURE OF PRE-EMPLOYMENT TRAINING

This form of training calls for (1) instruction in the ways of factory life, and (2) introduction to machines, tools and materials, and the acquiring of beginner's skill with a particular machine.

INSTRUCTION IN FACTORY WAYS

Among others, the following routines and practices should be stressed:

1) SAFETY

Safety should be emphasized from the very beginning for first impressions are lasting. The beginner should be taught the use of goggles, shields, and guards. His use of them where necessary should be stressed. He should be made acquainted with the destructive effect of centrifugal force as found in grinding wheels, fly wheels and work in machines. He should learn how to lift man loads safely and he should be schooled in the precautions to be taken against industrial hazards. Industrial hazards peculiar to the job and safeguards against them must be made clear. He should be informed about safety shoes and suitable work clothes.

2) SHOP INSTRUCTIONS

The prospective employee should understand the purpose of shop rules, booklets of information for employees, operation sheets, inspection forms and other printed material designed for control and report purposes and for informing the worker. He should learn how to punch a time clock, something about how the pay check is computed, and the prevailing methods of payment whether by check or in cash.

3) BLUE PRINTS AND MEASUREMENTS

If the factory job requires that a person work from blue prints, the course should include such instruction. Elementary shop mathematics may also be needed. The instruction should be practical; illustrations and problems should be drawn from the local industry for which the employee is being prepared.

4) MANUFACTURING PROCESS

An explanation of the flow of production through the shop is distinctly valuable. The description should refer to the industry in which the student is being trained, if that is possible. Production flow diagrams, assembly charts and similar exhibits that indicate graphically the steps in the production process are very helpful. Information about the ultimate use of the product is of value in creating and maintaining interest.

In order to gear the pre–employment and supplementary training into the manufacturing process, many of the school shops are laid out as nearly as possible to duplicate the production lines of war production plants and the training is given around the production of selected parts that may go into the final production assembly.

TRAINING IN USE OF MACHINES AND TOOLS

Training of this character should be specific—on the machine or with the tools that the student will subsequently use. A smattering of skill should be avoided. It is better that the beginner be able to perform one or two simple operations than that he be superficially acquainted with several.

Whenever possible, the shop facilities for instruction should approximate those in the factory where the prospective employee later will work. This refers especially to tools, machines, work benches and similar equipment. When this ideal cannot be realized, the next best equipment available should be provided. The suggestions below regarding instruction may be helpful:

1) MACHINES

When training prospective workers for the machine shop or a metal working establishment, the simple cutting operation on an engine lathe is of great value in acquainting the student with the workings of power driven tools. On this machine the student learns something about the process of cutting metal and about feeds and speeds. In addition, he becomes acquainted with cutting tools and how to grind them and the use of cutting solutions. He further grows familiar with the parts of the lathe and how to look after the machine. This experience is a good base for later training in various cutting operations. Engine lathes are available almost everywhere.

2) TOOLS

Correct practice in the use and care of these instruments of production should receive major attention. It is common knowledge that some losses in the plant are due to new workers who have not yet mastered the best methods of using simple tools and measuring instruments although they consider themselves competent. It is important that beginners receive early training in the correct use and care of small tools and instruments. Since they are available generally, a good deal of demonstration and practice may be afforded.

While in the school shop it is possible to develop a fair degree of dexterity in the use of calipers, snap and plug gauges and micrometers. This speeds the development of beginner's skill and discloses those who have mechanical aptitude.

3) MATERIALS

The beginner should learn something about the materials used in the industry for which he is being prepared. With samples at hand, their characteristics and applications can be demonstrated. Reference should be made also to solutions, lubricants, cleaners, finishers, abrasives, adhesives and so on.

AVAILABILITY OF PRE-EMPLOYMENT TRAINING

Pre–employment instruction in varying degree is available in almost every locality. Public vocational and trade schools, public high schools, and many of the engineering colleges are ready and willing to offer their services. In addition, government agencies, especially the NYA, consider the needs and recommendations of industry in shaping the content of their preemployment work projects.

SELECTION FOR PLACEMENT

While the primary object of pre–employment instruction is adjustment to the factory environment and the imparting of initial skill, this training should also reveal the individual employee's fitness for a job in industry.

Observation, instructor's ratings and performance records, together with a suitable testing method are helpful in grading the student with regard to general ability, speed of learning and capacity to handle jobs at various levels of skill. Information of this character is highly valuable to placement officers—in the schools, state employment office and local factories.

CONDITIONS FOR BEST RESULTS

The closer the cooperation between the plant and the school, the greater the likelihood of satisfactory placements and of success on the job. Being trained for a specific job and then being placed on that kind of work in a plant build confidence on the part of the new worker and aid in prompt adjustment to the working conditions.

HOW TO INSTRUCT A MAN ON THE JOB

14

Your supervisors have much instructing of workers to do. This instruction is important to the worker, the supervisor, you, your plant, and to national war production.

Perhaps these workers to be instructed have been with you for years or perhaps some have been transferred to your company—or many may be green—starting their first jobs.

Here are some ideas that will help your supervisors instruct their workers. They have been worked out by other supervisors who had the same job to do, just as the supervisors in your plant. They are easy to follow.

But—the supervisors, foremen, lead–men and gang bosses in your company will use this plan only as much as you demand that they use it. You cannot delegate orders for its use to others; you, the operating heads, are the ones who will make the use of this method accomplish real gains in the war production of your plant. It is YOUR responsibility to see they use it!

C. R. Dooley, Director
Training Within Industry

WHAT YOU WANT TO DO

Go back in your own memory. Remember how you felt the first day on a new job?—the time you were "stumped" by a new "wrinkle" on the job?—the time when you caused some scrap or re–work?—the time you got hurt?—the times when the boss corrected you and your work? Perhaps you liked the way he did it—or perhaps you didn't?

Any worker assigned to your supervisors feels the same way. He wants to make a good showing. You realize this. You are interested in four things:

1) Having the new worker come up to the quality and quantity requirements of production as quickly as possible.
2) Avoiding accidents which will injure the worker.
3) Avoiding damage to machines or equipment.
4) Spoiling as little work as possible.

Therefore, increasing the skill of supervision is a management responsibility.

HOW YOU CAN DO IT

Most of us just "jump right in" and start instructing or correcting a workman without much thought or planning. Perhaps your foremen do the same because:

They know the job so well they've forgotten the things that "stump" the learner.

They know it so well that they don't plan how to put it over.

They know it so well that they don't pick out the key points, the knacks—the things that cause accidents, scrap, re–work, delays, and damage to tools and equipment.

To instruct a man right takes just a little extra time at the moment, but it saves hours and days of time later on, and prevents a large part of the scrap, spoiled work and accidents. The following plan is simple and easy to follow. Furthermore, it works.

Before instructing, there are **FOUR GET READY POINTS** to watch.

They can be done in minutes.

When instructing, there are FOUR BASIC STEPS to follow. They really are no different than what your foremen may now be doing. But these steps help them do it *well* and *thoroughly*. At least they have helped thousands of others.

HOW TO GET READY TO INSTRUCT

Here are the **FOUR GET READY POINTS** which should be taken care of before instructing:

1) HAVE A TIME TABLE

- How much skill you expect him to have,
- By what date

When the pressure is heavy for production and men must be trained, common replies are, "IT TAKES TIME," or "A LOT OF MISTAKES ALWAYS HAPPEN," or "LET 'EM LEARN."

You can help production by making a Time Table for your workers. To make a TRAINING TIME TABLE, list the jobs under your supervision across the top of a sheet of paper and then list your workers' names down the left–hand side—check the jobs each worker can do, opposite his name.

Determine your IMMEDIATE TRAINING NEEDS in the light of turnover, performance, present work load, and future work load. Set yourself the dates when you will have trained your workers to fill these needs. *Time is short!*

Make and use a Time Table for yourself and your workers.

2) BREAK DOWN THE JOB

List the important steps—pick out the key points. (Safety is always a key point.) You know that there are a few "*key points*" in every operation that cause accidents, scrap, delays, and damage to tools and equipment. If these *key things* are done right, the whole operation is right. *If any one* of them is missed the operation is wrong.

- If you put the job over to the worker with these key points made clear, he will really "get it."
- He will do the operation right the *first time.*
- He won't be "fighting" the work—making mistakes getting hurt.

There is a quick, easy way to get the job clearly outlined in your mind. Fill out a "Breakdown Sheet" (sample enclosed) for any operations before you start to instruct the worker to do it. Do this on the job so that no key points will be overlooked. It only takes three to five minutes. This break-down is for your own use. It is not to be given to the worker.

3) HAVE EVERYTHING READY

- The right equipment, materials, and supplies.

When you so much as touch a job in front of a worker, set the *correct* example. Don't use the wrong tool. Don't fumble. Don't make excuses. Don't miss a trick. When *you* have everything right, *he* is more likely to do the same.

4) HAVE THE WORK PLACE PROPERLY ARRANGE

- just as the worker will be expected to keep it.

The same thing applies here as above. You must set the correct example. Put his bench, desk, stockpile, or wherever he is to work in proper order before you start to put over the job to him. *He* won't do it if *you* don't do it.

HOW TO INSTRUCT

Here is what you should do every time you instruct a man or correct his work:

STEP 1   PREPARE THE WORKER TO RECEIVE INSTRUCTION

- Put him at ease. Remember he can't think straight if you make him embarrassed or scared.

- State the job and find out what he already knows about it. Don't tell him things he already knows. Start in where his knowledge ends.

- Get him interested in learning the job. Relate his job or operation to the final production, so he knows his work is important.

- Place in correct position. Don't have him see the job backwards or from any other angle than that from which he will work.

STEP 2   PRESENT THE OPERATION

- Tell him, show him, illustrate, one IMPORTANT STEP at a time. Be patient—and go slowly. Get accuracy now, speed later.

- Stress the key points. Make them clear. These will make or break the operation—maybe make or break him.

- Instruct clearly, completely, and patiently—but no more than he can master. Put the instruction over in small doses. He (the same as all of us) can't catch but six or eight new ideas at one time and really understand them.

STEP 3   TRY OUT PERFORMANCE

- Have him do the job—correct errors. Don't bawl him out or indicate that he is "thick" or "dumb".

- Have him explain each KEY POINT to you as he does the job again. A lot of us find it easy to observe motions and not really understand what we are doing. YOU want him to UNDERSTAND.

- Make sure he understands.

- Continue until YOU know HE knows. He may have to do the job half a dozen times.

STEP 4   FOLLOW UP

- Put him on his own. Designate to whom he goes for help. Make this definite—yourself or someone you choose. The wrong person might give him a "bum steer."

- He has to get the feel of the job by doing it himself.

- Check frequently. Perhaps every few minutes at the start, to every few hours or few days later on. Be on the lookout for any incorrect or unnecessary moves. Be careful about your taking over the job too soon, or too often. Don't take it over at all if you can point out the help he needs.

- Taper off extra coaching and close follow–up until he is able to work under normal supervision.

Use this plan. You will find it amazing that such greatly improved results can come from such a simple plan.

Use it every time you need to put over a new operation, check a man's work, or change a work procedure.

IF THE WORKER HASN'T LEARNED
THE INSTRUCTOR HASN'T TAUGHT!

TRAINING PRODUCTION WORKERS

15

Many defense contractors are facing these common questions:

Where can I get skilled operators?
Is it too late to start training now?
Where can I train them?
How long does it take to get results?
Where can I get help on training plans?
How about the coat?
How should I start?

There are no stock answers to such questions which fit all localities or industries, but one defense contractor who had to answer them and triple his work force reports:

"As learners were 'broken in' on the day shifts, they were transferred to the second and third shifts and placed on their own. This kept up until all machines on all shifts were filled, resulting in a 24–hour day, 7–day week for the machines. Since the operators work a 5–day week, additional trained workers were made ready to take the places of the men who are off, to keep all machines running continuously.

"We found this system of training short and good; we know it will work in any industry and on any kind of work."

The following procedures represent successful practice in many leading companies. They are recommended to any company that wishes to get new workers into production in a minimum of training time and to develop experienced workers to their greatest usefulness.

C. R. Dooley, Director
Training Within Industry

EXPEDITING PRODUCTION THROUGH TRAINING

Three steps normally are taken in training production workers:
1) Engineer the jobs.
2) Instruct new workers on beginning jobs.
3) Instruct experienced workers in new skills.

These steps are such that any or all of them can be used and adapted to any company's production problem.

ENGINEERING THE JOBS

Some companies find it possible and advantageous to so engineer their producing facilities that each operation requires but one principal skill on the part of the worker to perform it.

Although the engineering of production processes may not seem to be a part of a training program, it does represent the first and basic step in meeting and simplifying the training problem because it sets up the steps to be followed in doing the work.

INSTRUCT NEW WORKERS ON BEGINNING JOBS

In most cases the surest, quickest and most thorough way to train a new man is *on–the–job,* where he does, or helps to do, productive work. This is true whether the new man has had no prior training; has perhaps learned beginning skills in a vocational school; has had prior experience in the field but in another industry; or possesses a skill that has not been used for some years, and must be brought up to date.

Through this plan, the principal features of which are given below, many companies have doubled their personnel and production in six months time.

Experienced operators from the various types of operations or machines, are selected to "break in" new men. Good "mechanics" do not necessarily make good teachers, so the selections are made with extreme care.

New operators are carefully selected. Tests, administered by someone familiar with their *limitations*, provide valuable aids to judgment.

A new man (several if the process permits) is placed with each experienced worker who has been selected to give the instruction. The more apt of the new men are placed on the more difficult operations.

The experienced operator gives the new man his initial job instruction and teaches him the entire operation as rapidly as he can master it. On many operations the help of the new man is such that production is increased, in which case the experienced operator may receive the benefit of such additional production in his pay. On others, there may be a temporary drop in production, in which case the experienced operator should receive extra compensation, i.e. beyond his reduced earnings, while engaged in instruction work.

This plan operates particularly well on jobs where there are several things to do, so that the experienced operator can keep the learner busy most of the time. Examples: machine tool operation, pipe fitting, boiler making. Where the job is a continuous series of repetitive operations, appropriate adaptation must be made. Examples: punching, drilling, stamping. Sometimes the new man can be put on the machine next to the experienced operator's machine.

Often it is necessary for the experienced operator to spend some time— from an hour to a day—with the new man getting him properly started.

Best results from this plan are obtained, of course, when the supervisory force understands the procedure and lends help and encouragement to both the experienced operators and the new men. The shop superintendent and all the supervisors should be familiar with the fundamental's of job analysis and also job instruction.

INSTRUCT EXPERIENCED WORKERS IN NEW SKILLS

This important phase of instruction on the job is one which is all too often overlooked. Many companies lose the full benefit of capable men, and many employees lose the opportunity to render their best service because no one takes the trouble to develop them to the maximum of their individual abilities.

The following are some of the many ways in which instruction may be given to experienced workers.

a. Through instruction or "coaching" by the foreman.

Here are just a few of the ways a foreman can help "bring a man along." Any foreman can use them if he is wide awake to his opportunities.

- Point out the important "tricks" or "knacks" of the job.

- Ask questions (tactfully, of course) regarding parts of the operation—where a certain part fits into the final product— why a tolerance is important to successful use—what would happen if certain mistakes are made.

- Explain technical and safety points through sketches that can be quickly drawn at the employees work place.

- Call operators from several interrelated operations together to inspect and review some scrapped material or faulty operation.

- Take or send operators to the final assembly line; to the department where their work is used; to the experimental or test department; or to wherever is necessary to gain a full understanding of the complete job.

b. *Through special instructors.*

Some companies have set up training sections separate from the regular production shop, using the output of such sections in the regular manufacturing process. Whether the instruction is given in production shops or in separate training sections, it is necessary to equip those selected to do the instructing with an organized knowledge of production operations and the ability to impart it to others. In some cases the number of men to be trained justifies making the experienced operator a full time instructor. (See Bulletin #2–B"How to Prepare Instructors to Give Intensive Job Instruction.")

c. *Through special arrangements so an employee can "get his hand in on new work."*

Sometimes it is possible for some of the machinery or equipment to be used after the close of the regular work shift by employees who wish to qualify for new jobs.

Where this is not possible, some companies put machinery and equipment in a special location expressly for the use of employees who wish to qualify for better jobs.

In each case, of course, a foreman or instructor is present, not only to instruct the employees thus engaged, but to assure that the equipment is properly used and left in proper condition for the next regular work shift or "practice group."

d. Through use of local schools.

Often vocational schools, high schools and engineering colleges can provide valuable help to experienced employees where there is machinery and equipment on which employees may practice higher skilled operations. These are effective to the extent that school and industry plan together and agree upon the instruction to be given.

It is equally important that a similar agreement be reached regarding related technical instruction to be given by the schools.

INCREASING WAR PRODUCTION THROUGH EMPLOYMENT OF WOMEN

16

Employing women in war industries in increasing numbers is inescapable, but should not be looked at as a substitute procedure. Employing a woman for any job that she can do, or can learn to do, will release a man either for work not suitable for women or for active armed service.

The employer who has never had any women employees on his force may need to be reminded, in some cases, that a new woman worker is just a new worker. Careful selection should furnish women who are good prospects—the same as men. New women need training—so do new men. They are entering a new environment, but so are farm hands who take factory jobs.

The place of women in industry has been well established since the last war. One–fourth of manufacturing workers are women, and a number are in technical or managerial fields. Employers who think that the employment of women introduces some mysterious element into the factory situation need to be reminded that they have known women all their lives—secretaries, nurses, waitresses, saleswomen—and that women from all these groups will inevitably become a part of the war production effort.

This bulletin draws on the experience of a number of industries where women workers have had an important part for many years, and on the experience of British war production.

C. R. Dooley, Director
Training Within Industry

WOMEN IN THE LABOR SUPPLY PICTURE

In many industrial centers there already are labor shortages. In general, women will not add to the supply of skilled labor, but they do present a large and promising source of workers for a wide variety of operations. In England it has been necessary to require young women to take part in the war effort, either through auxiliary service or actual productive work in factories. There are many women who now need to earn wages. Curtailment of civilian production releases numbers of women with varying degrees of skill. These women are available for retraining for war production work.

SPECIAL FACTORS TO CONSIDER IN EMPLOYING WOMEN

Introduction of women workers in industries or plants where they have not previously been employed will often mean that women will actually be put on "merits work." It will not always be a simple placement and training process—but, when the snags are anticipated, British experience shows that remarkable results are achieved. Management needs to give advances and immediate consideration to some general facts—some limitations, some advantages, and some changes in facilities and equipment.

STATE LAWS REGARDING WOMEN WORKERS

Many states have "protective" legislation which sets standards for working conditions for women, limits hours (both as to length and time of day), and restricts occupations. In some states provisions have been made to permit modification of standards where necessary for war production. State laws covering a particular plant should be checked as the first step. The Industrial Commission or the State Secretary of Labor can supply specific information.

PHYSICAL LIMITATIONS OF WOMEN WORKERS

There are some physical limitations for women. As a means of overcoming them, mechanical aids may be used—for example, in load–lifting, roller conveyors and pedestal lifts are helpful. Tools may need to be scaled to women and benches made lower for assembly workers.

SAFETY AND THE WOMAN WORKER

The safety records of women are better than those of men, but there are special hazards to be recognized. It may be necessary to require the wearing of protective clothing. The safety engineer who selects caps and jumpers will do well to consult with the women who will wear the clothing—his interest may be in finding a cap which will insure that hair will not catch in a machine, while the employee may also be concerned about a cap which will protect hair from dust and not ruin a new hair–do. It is poor practice to select clothing which requires disciplinary action to enforce wearing or which causes resentment.

ABSENCE RECORDS

Women's records for days–off are worse than men's. They are not altogether due to illness but frequently to unavoidable home responsibilities. A "flying squadron" of utility operators who can fill in on numerous jobs is a common solution.

LABOR TURNOVER

Women do not change jobs as often as men. Good supervision, satisfactory working conditions, adequate wages, and fair treatment will hold women to their jobs and thus, by decreased turnover, reduce overall training time.

SUPERVISION

Many persons will advocate the employment of a woman personnel officer to work on problems connected with working women. This is based on the assumption that there is an innate and intangible difference between men and women as employees that will be beyond a man's experience. This is not the best basis for the introduction of women to the production shop. Women are entering war production on the same terms as men, even if it is necessary to make physical segregation in a few respects and to separate groups in individual situations. Their relation to the personnel department is the same as new men. Women have a useful place in personnel offices, but not necessarily as concerned with women employees.

The woman who is new as a factory employee is making a change. Skilled personnel people should handle cases relating to people new to industrial situations.

Women as first-line supervisors can sometimes handle routine departmental problems concerning women more easily than men, and women can train women. The opening of even minor supervisory positions to women will provide a promotion incentive. However, if women supervisors do not correspond in authority with men in similar positions, the employees may be inclined to by-pass the woman supervisor and take their problems to the man whom they feel is "the boss."

SELECTION AND PLACEMENT OF WOMEN WORKERS

All women will not, of course, make productive factory employees. The selection procedure should include particular attention to the background brought to the job—education, training, and aptitudes. The housewife who is untrained and perhaps free for only part-time work may move into civilian production and service operations, releasing for full-time war production employment, women who have had regular work experience.

Even in the comparatively short time of current war production, there are a number of instances of the value of certain backgrounds of work requiring deft hands—girls who were needle workers or hairdressers have proved specially adaptable for precision metal work. With good training, they work to tolerances measured in ten-thousandths of an inch. Jobs requiring "feel," such as minute assembly and adjustment, are examples of jobs where placement of women has produced particularly good results, in many instances better than men.

A common opinion is, "Women have no mechanical ability." It is more accurate to say that they have little "mechanical familiarity." Women are not accustomed to working with wrenches and drills, but the lowered level at which training begins also means an opportunity to begin training with correct procedures—they do not bring "picked-up" bad habits to the job.

TRAINING FOR WOMEN THE SAME AS FOR MEN

Well-planned training for women who have been selected and placed according to good standards will provide a large, productive new force and give perfectly satisfactory results in every respect.

GET READY FOR THE JOB. What is the work? Should it be broken up into several jobs, to be taught separately?

CONSIDER THE WORK PLACE, THE TOOLS. Are changes needed?

FIND OUT WHAT THE NEW WORKERS ALREADY KNOW. Is some preliminary instruction needed in shop arithmetic or blueprint reading? Would advance familiarity with small tools help? Will "shop terms and procedures" need special explanation? What pre-employment training is available?

TRAIN ON THE JOB. Does instruction given on the job include supervised tryout and follow up? Does the new employee know where to go for help?

PROVIDE SUPPLEMENTARY INSTRUCTION. Does the plant provide training to round–out background and increase skills? Are there public vocational courses available?

UPGRADE TO HIGHER SKILLS. Are women being moved on to more difficult jobs as they show ability, in order to make maximum use of their best skills?

JOBS FOR WOMEN IN WAR INDUSTRY

To turn again to British experience, women are working successfully on these jobs:

assembly	lathe work
band–sawing	boring
optical grinding/polishing	crane operation
press operating	drilling
riveting	turning

To summarize the overall problem, the contractor must:

1) Consider the employment of women with an open mind.

2) Recognize that there is, as always, a training job to do.

INTRODUCING THE NEW EMPLOYEE TO THE JOB

17

THE IMPORTANCE OF A GOOD INTRODUCTION

A new place to work means adjustment for any individual. It is easy for the new man to jump to wrong conclusions. The supervisor has an excellent chance, during this impressionable period, to establish a good relationship with the employee and see that he gets accurate information about the place where he is working. He can get the new man off to the right start.

This process of making the new employee feel at home, often called induction, goes on at the same time as job instruction, and both have the same aim—making the new man a productive part of the business. It should not be assumed that instruction will do both jobs. The success of instruction may depend on the quality of the introduction process.

C. R. Dooley, Director
Training Within Industry

PROCESS OF INTRODUCING EMPLOYEES

Some of the questions that arise in introducing employees are: Can all employees be inducted alike? What attention should be given to a transferred or rehired employee compared to the new employee? Is a systemized plan desirable? Many of these questions can be answered only in terms of conditions in the organization. In general, however, the process of introduction can be considered under these headings:

1) handling the initial interview

2) providing the employee with company information

3) providing the employee with information about his work

4) assisting the employee to adjust to his fellow–workers

These phases of the introduction process are interrelated and, therefore, should be regarded just as a sequence of steps. As a reminder of the information to be given and to enable the supervisor to know what he has covered when it is necessary to contact the employee at intervals, a checklist may be provided (see Exhibit A at end of bulletin).

1. HANDLING THE INITIAL INTERVIEW — The supervisor's first approach to the employee will have considerable influence on his future attitude toward the supervisor and the company. The supervisor should draw upon his experience in dealing with men and be careful to see that he does not make statements and actions which can be misinterpreted. The supervisor should use this opportunity to begin to establish a friendly attitude which, of course, should carry over beyond the induction period.

Many supervisors follow these interviewing steps:

a) Beforehand, the supervisor considers what he already knows about the new employee and tries to picture how he would feel if he were in his shoes. His objective is to make the employee feel that in him he has a supervisor who will consider impartially but sympathetically whatever problem he may care to talk over.

b) If conditions make it possible, the new employee is brought to the supervisor's desk where he is greeted and asked to sit down. In any event, the best conditions for an uninterrupted interview are sought.

c) To arrive at common ground and establish mutual interests, the employee is asked a question or two on matters of general interest. This usually gets the employee to talking and enables the supervisor to learn more about him without appearing inquisitive. He may have to try several different tacks to establish a mutual understanding and avoid putting the employee on the defensive.

d) The supervisor decides the proper time to start giving the employee information about the company and the employee's job. The employee himself may lead into this through questions.

e) In closing the interview the supervisor should leave the employee feeling that he can come back at any time.

2. PROVIDING THE EMPLOYEE WITH INFORMATION ABOUT THE COMPANY IN WHICH HE WORKS

—The employee must be provided with accurate information about the company and its policies, as early as practicable after he reports to work, in small enough segments to be retained. It is desirable to see him several times at intervals during the first two or three days. One of the main considerations is to cause the employee to feel proud of the company and to give him an appreciation of its policies and what they mean to him. The new employee should be urged, when he wants to know more, to come to the same source for information—the first-line supervisor.

When possible, some information should be given to the employee by his department chief, in order to widen the employee's knowledge of the organization and to give the department chief an additional way of knowing his people. It also provides the chief with an opportunity for checking the introduction of the employee. There should, however, be an understanding among those concerned as to precisely what information the department chief will give the employee. It is desirable for the department chief to provide that information on which it is desired to place special emphasis.

The supervisor is the best judge of the extent to which he should make a detailed explanation of any one item. Ordinarily the broad objectives of the company programs, what they mean to the employee, and how he can take advantage of them, will suffice. Care should be exercised to see that the employee does not feel subjected to pressure to participate in company social or service activities.

3. PROVIDING THE EMPLOYEE WITH INFORMATION ABOUT HIS WORK

—A distinction should be made between this phase of the induction process and job instruction. The objective here is to assist the employee to adjust to his new situation through providing him with background information. Much of this information, of course, such as location of the lockers, will have to be given shortly after he reports for work. Information about work is of immediate concern, and should be given clearly. If he is new to the job he may be unfamiliar with terminology. He should be encouraged to ask questions. Most new employees want to make a good impression and are afraid of not "catching on" rapidly.

4. ASSISTING THE EMPLOYEE TO ADJUST HIMSELF TO HIS FELLOW WORKERS

—Most individuals who are new to an organization are concerned over how they will be accepted by their fellow-workers. Getting off to the right start with fellow-workers depends greatly upon the employee himself, but the supervisor can see that the new employee is introduced to those in the vicinity of his work and, in some instances, it may be desirable to tell the employee a few interesting things about his fellow-workers. When it is possible to make a choice of several work locations for the new employee, the supervisor can give considerations to the interests, sex, age, and other characteristics of those near whom he might be placed. It might, in a few instances, even be desirable to change a seating arrangement so that the new employee will be located in a group where he will get along satisfactorily.

Most supervisors, through knowing their people, develop a "feel" for such conditions. Helping the employee adjust to his working group will not ordinarily be done by one single action, but will involve many follow–ups over a considerable period of time. It has been said, probably rightly, that the supervisor's work in helping employees adjust to each other is never finished.

SYSTEMIZING THE INTRODUCTION PROCESS

When new employees are being taken into an organization, some systemized procedure should be adopted. This may involve doing certain things on certain days, or it may be nothing more than delegating responsibility for inducting the new employee.

For any induction procedure, a plan is wise—and it must be a plan made from the viewpoint of the man with his needs in mind. These points should be considered:

PURPOSE
    1. What should the new employee get from the introduction process?
    2. What should the company get?

CONTENT
    1. What routines and regulations must be explained at once? Which later?
    2. What company information must be given?

METHOD
    1. Is process on individual or group basis?
    2. Will a plant or department trip be included?

RESPONSIBILITY
    1. What is supervisor's part?
    2. What is employment office's part?
    3. Who will coordinate and check complete coverage?

TIMING
    1. What is the order in which information is to be given?
    2. How much shall be given at one time?

By using the guide which appears as Exhibit A on page 106 as a check–list for the kind of information to be given the employee, a plan suitable to the organization can be worked out in a short time. Such a plan can probably be best prepared through the collaborative efforts of the supervisors in the department where it is to be used. A detailed time schedule, such as Exhibit B on page 107, may be desirable.

After a guide has been drawn up, it is good practice to set down the elementary information needed. For example, not until the new man knows the location of the time–clock, how it is operated, where to put his card, the occasions on which he is required to register, the rules about registering only his own card, and what to do if he makes a mistake, can the subject of time–clocks be considered adequately covered.

It has been estimated that from six to twelve hours is needed to provide the employee with basic information about the company and his job. It is obvious that, if many new employees are coming to the plant, supervisors may not have this much time to give to many employees individually. Although personal contact with the new employee is highly desirable, it may be necessary during such periods to use group methods to convey some of the information about the company and the employee's work to new employees. Regardless of the number of new employees, however, the supervisor should not fail to make some personal contact with each of them as early as possible, doing what he can to assist them in feeling at home.

INDUCTING THE TRANSFERRED OR REHIRED EMPLOYEE

It is obvious that neither as much information nor attention will ordinarily have to be given to the rehired or transferred employee as to the newly hired employee. Sometimes there is a failure to explain clearly to an employee the reasons for his transfer, an item of great concern to him. Although his former supervisors and the employment office are responsible, his new supervisor can well afford to make sure that he understands, and that any doubts he may have are expressed and talked over as early as possible. It should be remembered that this employee will have to pass through an adjusting or orienting period similar to the new employee. Supervisors should not take it for granted that these employees are familiar with the company or their work, yet to assume they are totally ignorant of the organization may provoke resentment. In addition to these general kinds of information, the rehired or transferred employee usually wants to know, promptly, what grade of work he is assigned to, what his rate and probable earnings will be, what shift he is to be working, and similar information that shows him at once "where he stands."

SUMMARY

Introducing an employee means that the supervisor obtains background information about the man as well as giving him information and assistance. The supervisor needs to know his men, and the man needs to know the department so that he will feel at home. It is during this period of adjustment that the employee's future worth to the company is largely determined. The employee's immediate supervisor should see that this is done regardless of whether complete authority has been delegated to him or a systemized plan, involving the employment office, has been adopted. The supervisor's success in introducing employees will depend largely on the care and insight with which he approaches this work. His experience in dealing with people should be constantly drawn upon for help.

Employee Hire Date	Information given by	Date
1. Has he read the employee handbook?		
2. Does he know safety rules, practices, and the reporting of accidents? Where to get first–aid treatment? Has he read the safety handbook?		
3. Have factory regulations—smoking, fire drills, absences, etc.—been explained?		
4. Does he know location of lockers and washrooms?		
5. Does he know location of cafeteria? Lunch, rest–period times?		
6. Was he informed about time–clock and clock–card rules?		
7. Does he know about passes—temporary, permanent, package?		
8. Does he know organization of department, division, and shop? Names of supervisors?		
9. Does he know what the department manufacturers?		
10. Has he been introduced to fellow–workers and told about company activities?		
11. Have company personnel policies been explained?		
12. Does he know how his pay is figured: piece–rate, incentives, learning period, overtime, payroll, deductions, etc.?		
13. Does he understand the benefit or insurance plan?		
14. Does he know where to get information? Help?		

Exhibit B
Induction outline

When & Where?	What & How?	By Whom?
First Day 1. On arrival in plant	1. Introduction to working supervisor	1. By person who did the hiring

2. On arrival in department 15 minutes	2. Information needed in daily routine
	  a. Any information he may need on getting to and from work, parking regulations, etc.
	  b. Starting time, lunch period, quitting time, hours per week
	  c. Review of compensation items (when he will be paid, where, how, how much)
	  d. Opportunity for questions
		2. By supervisor

3. Following preliminary interview. One half hour	3. Meeting other workers, getting to know layout of building
	  a. Trip through department with general explanation of product
	  b. Show him where he is to work and meet neighboring workers.
	  c. Show him his locker and location of wash rooms.
	  d. Show him the time–clock, his card, and explain regulations.
	  e. Tell him about any special rules on smoking, leaving department, etc.
		3. By supervisor or group leader

4. Following till noon	4. Job Instruction	4. By person who is to handle training

5. Noon	5. Show location of cafeteria and eat lunch with new man.
	  a. Show him noon recreation facilities.
	  b. Introduce him to others.
		5. Neighboring worker

6. After lunch till half hour before quitting time	6. Job Instruction	6. Trainer

When & Where?	What & How?	By Whom?
7. Half hour before closing	7. Give pass, explain use, and regulation in case of absence. Give booklet of rules, regulations, and policies to be read at home.	7. Supervisor

Second Day
 	
1. At a convenient time, one half hour
	1. Review booklet of rules and regulations, policies.
	   a. to see that he understands subjects covered in booklet
	   b. to give opportunity to ask questions
		1. Supervisor

2. At a convenient time, 15 minutes	2. Check through job with safety engineer and review policies and procedures on safety.	2. Safety Engineer

Within First Week	1. Meet with other new men from other departments
	   a. Tour plant
	   b. Have organization set–up described
	   c. Have mutual benefit and other organization plans described
		1. Personnel Department

Fifth Day	1. Interview with supervisor of job
	   a. Find out what he is thinking
	   b. Clear up any misunderstanding
	   c. Give the opportunity for questions
		1. Supervisor

SAFETY ON THE JOB FOR THE NEW EMPLOYEE

18

Industrial safety is vital to war production. All accidents interfere with the flow of work; many result in damage to machinery, equipment, or work; some involve injuries. Injuries result in at least temporary loss of services when full–time work of every employee is needed.

It is important that the new employee receive an early introduction to the company's program and policies in relation to safety. *The right way to do a job is the safe way, and training in the right way to do a job will be training in the safe way to work.* Safety must be an integral part of the introducing and instructing process.

If safety is handled as an "after–thought," either in induction or instruction, the employee may consider it as apart from his regular duties. Safety is not something just for a meeting, not just a humane attitude—it is fundamental in getting out maximum war production.

This bulletin has been prepared with the cooperation of the National Committee for the Conservation of Manpower in War Industries, Division of Labor Standards, United States Department of Labor.

C. R. Dooley, Director
Training Within Industry

INTRODUCING EMPLOYEES TO SAFETY

Introduction to safety is part of job induction. The program and policy of the company, its safety rules and regulations, must be put over in the general introduction so as to form a natural part of the particular job under consideration.

1) HANDLING THE INITIAL INTERVIEW

The supervisor should always take into account the man's previous experience. If this is his first job—what, if anything, does he probably know about industrial safety in general? If he received training at a trade or vocational school—what attention, if any, was paid to safe work practices? If he has been employed in another company, what safety program does that company have? What was the employee's injury record? If these facts are not known beforehand, the supervisor should attempt to draw them out during the interview.

2) PROVIDING EMPLOYEES WITH INFORMATION ABOUT THE COMPANY SAFETY PROGRAM

Information concerning the company's safety program and policies should be given at the same time as information concerning general policies.

Stress the measures to guard machines and minimize physical hazards, as well as management's interest in the workers' well–being.

3) PROVIDING THE EMPLOYEE WITH INFORMATION ABOUT SAFETY AT HIS WORK

When the employee is being given information about his work, point out the hazards to which he will be exposed; (a) in the type of work to which he will be assigned; (b) as a result of work being performed in his immediate vicinity; and (c) as a result of operations or processes carried on in the department. The supervisor should stress the precautions which the employee must take to avoid injury, and *emphasize individual responsibility* for safety and the advantage to the employee.

The supervisor should also point out the dangers attendant upon "horse play" and the unauthorized use or the misuse of air hose and other equipment. Company rules should be explained clearly.

The employee should be given general information about any plant safety contests or campaigns, and the standing of his department in them. General safety measures, such as type of clothing, rules for keeping aisle ways clear, enclosures around belts, storage and piling of materials and equipment, should be pointed out during the tour of the department. If the safeguard or rule was adopted following a serious accident, or if an accident has resulted from disregard of safety, mention the incident when the guard or rule is pointed out. The employee should be shown the first aid room, and have explained to him rules concerning the reporting of even "trivial" injuries.

4) SAFETY IN "HAZARDOUS" PLANTS

In many war production plants conditions should frankly be described the employee as "hazardous." Make the distinction between "dangerous" and "hazardous." Where explosions can be caused by carelessness, only the thorough following of a rigid safety program can keep a hazardous plant from being a dangerous one.

If accident probability is high, more restrictions may be necessary. For example, employees may be permitted to move about only in their working area, and clothing may be designed because of special hazards.

5) RESPONSIBILITY FOR INTRODUCTORY MATERIAL ON SAFETY

The safety performance of the new employee, like his work performance, is the responsibility of his supervisor. A safety program, supervised by a safety engineer, does not excuse the supervisor any more than an regionalized plan of induction justifies failure to follow through on the general induction process. As in the whole induction process, the supervisor's care and insight in approaching the job, and his experience in dealing with people, will determine the success or failure of the introduction to safety.

SAFETY AND THE TRANSFERRED OR REHIRED EMPLOYEE

When an employee enters a new department, he needs safety information and training to almost the degree of the new man. He may know the company's general policy, but he needs information about his new assignment. The new department probably will have its own rules and hazards. If a bad accident record figured in reasons for a lay-off, previous discharge, or transfer, stress safety rules and regulations particularly.

SAFETY IN INSTRUCTION

A good job breakdown must be made before good job instruction can begin. A job breakdown shows how to do the job efficiently, *safely*, economically. The safe practices in a job are true key points. There are short cuts on most jobs, but speed on one piece of work is not as important on war production as is continuous output. Safety and efficiency are simultaneous products of good machine design, well planned processes, and carefully thought-out work practices. Good job breakdowns and thorough training are foundations for safe, efficient work.

THE PLANT SAFETY PROGRAM

In many localities, safety has suffered from a sentimental approach. Management may feel that its job is handled by the statement that unsafe practices will not be tolerated." Some companies look on safety as a public relations policy (a few believe that a plant safety program ranks along with factory picnics—devices to build good will).

SAFETY AND PRODUCTION

Safety *is* a production problem. Every accident, whether or not it involves human injury, is an interruption to the orderly flow of production. Manpower loss is a block to production which is almost impossible to make up. Planning instruction on the basis of the safe way and emphasizing hazards along with key points in breaking in a man on a new job are realistic foundations for a plant safety program which is undertaken on the basis of good business in war time," not just because "it's the right thing to do."

Safety is a continuous job—it is necessary to follow up constantly to make sure that the man whose speed is increasing is not making time through dangerous short–cuts. Such short–cuts, though spectacular at the moment, will not speed production. Short–cuts may point out the need for a better way to do a job—but a shorter way cannot be tolerated unless it is safe.

Planning for safety may be a staff job, and the design and installation of safety equipment is definitely work for a safety engineer, but making safety effective in the plant is an integral part of the job of line supervisors. (Safety engineers and foremen can get training in safety methods through courses in Safety Engineering Defense Training, offered by engineering colleges and sponsored by the National Committee for the Conservation of Manpower in War Industries and the U. S. Office of Education. Tuition is paid by the Office of Education.)

SAFE PRACTICES

Do not depend on the making out of an elaborate set of safety rules. Sometimes regulations are an invitation to breaking them. "Safe practices"—the right way to do the job, illustrated on the job—will overcome this difficulty in many cases. Safe practices have to be worked out for specific jobs. Some belong to the factory, or perhaps to the industry as a whole, but most are at the job level. Safe practices are the natural outgrowth of good job instruction.

GROUP APPROACH

Posters and meetings where generalities are the topic do not put safety across. Reminders can be useful if a ground–work has been laid, but they cannot do the whole job. Poorly planned contests may only result in rivalry which promotes records, but does not improve conditions and may even lead to failure to report accidents. To obtain results a safety program must have whole–hearted management backing; and, to hold interest, it must provide for active employee participation. Group instruction in safety is effective when it is keyed to specific practices and hazards which are within the job experience. The foreman who studies his department's safety records and knows the causes of accidents can promote safety effectively. Specific hazards should be emphasized continuously—the hazards exists even in an accident–free period.

GUARDS

Mechanical guards are safety devices only when they are used. Installation of guards, and then depending on them to do the whole job, is acutely dangerous. Half–hearted enforcement of such regulations as those about wearing goggles can lead to contempt for a whole safety program. No equipment should be specified without good reasons, and the reasons should be explained to all employees involved. Once made and explained, the regulation must be enforced.

SAFETY AND HEALTH

Many jobs demand attention, good vision, strength, or other definite physical requirements. Regular physical examinations are as important as are checks on the condition of mechanical equipment.

SAFETY CLOTHING

Safety clothing is designed for several purposes: (a) to make the new worker conspicuous (some companies require new employees to wear red caps so that those with more experience will watch out to assist the new people); (b) to protect the employee by guarding against the possibility of having hair or loose clothing caught in moving machinery, or having feet hurt by falling objects (safety shoes are invaluable in accident prevention); (c) to protect other employees (in this group are the garments which are free from metal or other material which might cause accident).

SUMMARY

To put over safety for the new man as well as the experienced employee:

1) Be clear—and give the reasons.

2) Be business–like—not sentimental.

3) Be reasonable in making rules—but firm in enforcing.

4) Insist that supervisors set the example in safe practices.

TRAINING WORKERS TO MEET DEFENSE NEEDS

1 9

The rapidly increasing need for more training on the job in Defense plants calls for a common understanding of training objectives.

During this emergency we must keep our eyes on the one common objective—much more production in the shortest possible time. With the unanimous approval of the Labor Division's *Advisory Committee on Training*, the following statement of policy is issued for the information of workers and management.

This bulletin is supplemented by two others. One of these is Bulletin 1—The Training within Industry Program—which outlines measures for giving effect to the policies described. The other is Bulletin 1–A—Organization and Personnel, which lists those who are charged with putting the policies and program to work throughout industry. Other bulletins issued by this branch take up various phases of training most essential to Defense.

C. R. Dooley, Chief
Training Within Industry

LEARN BY DOING—PRODUCE WHILE LEARNING

In this emergency, as well as in more normal times, it is good American practice and efficient business to have each worker make the fullest use of his best skill up to the maximum of his individual ability. Only through such use of the intelligence and skill of the nation's man-power will production keep pace with defense needs.

1) Additional workers will not be trained unless the available unemployed of equal skill have been absorbed or none are available locally.

2) There are normal losses from among skilled workers due to advancement into supervisory positions, changes to other occupations, sickness, death and retirement. These losses go on continuously, and it is necessary to bring along well trained workers to replace them. In addition, there is need to make up for the lack of apprentice training during the past ten years. These are the reasons why organized apprenticeship programs are so important now.

There are two important phases of apprentice training:

> Definitely planned program of experience, scheduled and assigned step by step to enable the apprentice over a pre-determined time to acquire skill on increasingly difficult kinds of work in a trade.

> For every skilled job there is related technical matter, much of which can best be taught off the job. To be effective, this related instruction must be very closely tied into the current job experience. Practice, related theory and technical knowledge must go hand in hand. Workers, employers and technical educators should collaborate in determining what shall be included in this instruction and how it can best be related to the work experience.

The proportion of apprentices to be trained can best be determined in local areas in numbers and programs agreed upon in joint conferences between management and interested groups of employees or by agreements arrived at by collective bargaining units.

3) In a less formal way, many workers acquire a breadth of experience by

learning one job at a time and becoming skilled in that, and advancing to a higher grade of work when opportunity permits. In an upgrading program the time cannot be definite and is controlled by available opportunities, depending upon production programs and specific vacancies as they occur. This differs from an apprenticeship program where the opportunity is controlled by advance agreement. Therefore, while craftsman experience may be gained by an apprentice in from three to four years, it may take the production specialist two or three times as long, or longer, to acquire corresponding skill and versatility through an upgrading program.

In times of rapid expansion when there is a shortage of skilled workers, there is no choice but that of using inexperienced workers from other kinds of work or young people without any work experience but with good orientation background gained in public vocational schools during pre–employment training. Through intensive instruction they then must be brought to their highest skill on a limited operation in the shortest possible time. Advancement into more skilled work should always be made from among employees of longer experience on jobs which are good foundations for the higher skills. Attempts should not be made to replace skilled workers by narrowly skilled specialists.

This puts upon Management a two–fold responsibility:

> Foremen, instructors and experienced workers must assist less experienced workers in acquiring new skills, and ....

> They should see that employees who have the desire and capacity for advancement be not kept indefinitely on jobs requiring skill in single operations.

4) Apprenticeship, upgrading, and supervisory training programs within industry are greatly implemented by making available opportunities for individuals to get instruction and related knowledge which enable them to fit themselves for advancements. Whether these facilities are made available by public educational institutions, employers, or organized labor groups, it is essential that there be continuous consultation between students, management, and educators. Only through such cooperation can the instruction be of immediate practical value.

Such philosophy, such practices, and such consultation should result in well–balanced training programs, and bring about an orderly and an effective approach to creating and maintaining a supply of competent workers available to meet the rapidly increasing needs of defense industry.

UPGRADING

20

This bulletin outlines a practice which is probably more widely used throughout American industry than any other form of industrial training, and which is most important from the standpoint of both production and employees. Many companies have long pursued excellent programs of "upgrading" without ever having given the practice a name. Now is the time for every company to review its upgrading practice.

Jobs are not static—they are lines of flow through the shop. One job leads to a better one, and, step by step, the employee receives his training and advances in skill. The job is a rung on the ladder of progress—this is the efficient way as well as the American way. Upgrading is a method that leads workers upward in the pyramid of organization. Rapid and efficient training can be made to meet unusual needs through such a definite step–by–step program.

C. R. Dooley, Director
Training Within Industry

WHAT UPGRADING IS

Upgrading refers to the natural and logical movement of employees within an organization for the purpose of developing and using each to the maximum of his abilities. Specifically, upgrading means:

1) DEFINITE LINES OF PROGRESSION—

planned promotion from within, both in departments and between departments

transfer to work for which a worker is best fitted, or to other lines of work where greater opportunity lies having qualified employees "trade jobs" to develop experience and versatility— "job rotation"

2) JOB INSTRUCTION—

instructing employees rather than "letting them learn" when promoted or transferred

3) RATE ADJUSTMENTS—

prompt adjustments in individual rates, according to performance on the job and movement to other jobs—periodic rate review to assure equity

4) SUPPLEMENTARY INSTRUCTION—

encouraging employees to pursue related outside instruction to increase usefulness

WHY UPGRADING IS SO IMPORTANT

From the company's standpoint the development of each employee to his highest level of usefulness is requisite to company success. Building competent manpower is considered one of management's primary functions in many companies.

From the employee's standpoint, growth and advancement through his work should represent the central core of his life.

Nothing is so destructive to employee efficiency, loyalty, and morale as to have a man hired from the outside and given a higher rated job for which someone already employed feels he could qualify. Telling the worker that the pressure of war production is so great that there is no time to give him the opportunity to learn another job is not a satisfactory answer. This is especially true in the case of a man who has his eye on a better job.

Furthermore, when an employee understands that upgrading is an established policy, he will do a better job of "breaking in" a new worker assigned to him.

When pressure for production eases and retrenchment becomes imminent, worker efficiency and loyalty will perhaps be even more necessary. It is essential, therefore, that the foundations for good future industrial relations be laid now.

HOW UPGRADING IS DONE

A well–rounded program of upgrading includes the following practices:

DETERMINE POLICY

Top management issues a written policy or letter clearly stating that vacancies are to be filled by upgrading, promoting, transferring, or rotating present workers before new workers are hired. All new workers are thus hired for certain definite beginners' jobs in the low paid brackets.

PLAN THE PROGRAM

One individual who is familiar with jobs and workers in the plant is assigned the task of collaborating with superintendents and foremen in preparing a plan by which the upgrading is to be done. In a small plant the program may be both planned and carried out by the superintendent—but the important feature is that one person must draw up a schedule of orderly movement from job to job. There are certain steps which fit the operation, whether the scale is large or small:

1) **DETERMINE LINES OF PROGRESSION (FROM WHAT JOB TO WHAT JOB).** Usually it is found that there are many groups of operations for which there already are natural lines of promotion. There are others, however, that do not fit into the normal promotional sequence and which *should* be fitted into the sequence to provide normal promotional opportunity and to prevent them from becoming "blind alley" jobs.

   All production jobs in the shop are listed in the order which indicates the lines of promotion from the lowest rated to the highest rated. This is done by departments, occupations, or any logical grouping of jobs. In many cases this means movement from one department to another; for example, machine operator to apprentice toolmaker, toolmaker to tool design engineer.

   Of course "line of progression" does not mean that movement from each job to the next is an immediate promotion. Obviously, before a promotion to many jobs is possible, workers may be transferred to two or more jobs on the present level to prepare them for promotion. Perhaps two, three, or more workers are asked to trade jobs to give them necessary background and work experience. (Occasionally this means that a worker must temporarily move to a *lower rated job* in order to get into a different line of work where eventually he can move up the line and into higher earnings.)

The line of promotion indicates *the order in which jobs must be learned,* so that, if this learning order is followed over a period of time, each worker will be using his best skill to the maximum of his individual ability.

2) INDICATE EXPERIENCE NECESSARY TO QUALIFY THE EMPLOYEE FOR EACH JOB. For each job, the operations that a qualified operator must be able to perform should be indicated. Such descriptions provide a ready reference for busy superintendents and foremen when promotions are considered, and are particularly helpful when transfers or rotations are planned for workers who need additional experience and "rounding out" before qualifying for promotion.

This work can be completed in a short time and requires only brief attention from time to time to keep up to date as jobs change. Descriptions should be charted and distributed to all shop supervisors as changes are made.

3) DETERMINE WHERE JOB ROTATION IS APPLICABLE. In those departments where all the employees perform work substantially of like difficulty, and where there are no "lines of promotion," about the only upgrading that can be done is job rotation. The benefits of this practice to employees and to the company will vary according to the kind of operation.

Job rotation is particularly useful in companies having frequent rush orders, emergencies, rapid expansions or seasonal fluctuations, engineering, and model changes. To meet these problems promptly and efficiently, a flexible and versatile work force is highly desirable. The more jobs each employee can perform, the more useful he is under a wide variety of conditions.

Some workers do not want to move, do not want to be "upgraded;" others are anxious to master new skills. A program of job rotation is a good way to discover those employees who can learn several jobs, do so quickly and who have enterprise and initiative.

ASSIGN RESPONSIBILITY

Line superintendents and foremen, of course, are held responsible for carrying out the program.

The responsibility for *helping* them carry out the upgrading program is delegated to the individual who has done most of the work in planning it. This is a full–time job in large plants and part–time in small ones. He is given authority to suggest, to foremen and others, advantageous moves of workers, and he must be consulted and be in agreement with any promotions or transfers to be made. Any disagreement between the upgrading planning man and the superintendents or foremen moves up the line for review and final decision by a top executive.

SEE THAT THE PLAN IS CARRIED OUT

A top executive keeps *personal* touch with a control of the upgrading program during the early weeks. He approves employment of new workers only after shop superintendents and others have shown him in detail that every present worker who is qualified for a better job has been promoted and that all other logical and reasonable transfers to round out experience have been made.

This personal control is maintained only for such time as is necessary to assure that the policy is definitely understood and consistently carried out throughout the organization.

SELECT QUALIFIED EMPLOYEES FOR UPGRADING

When better jobs are open, they should be filled by the best qualified employees. An inventory of the working force will classify the employee's potential ability, previous experience, education, his job preference, and length of service. No matter what form this inventory takes—whether through interviews or personnel records or any other means—such information is essential to upgrading.

Such a centrally controlled plan makes available, for quick reference, information about qualifications of individual workers, job requirements, and paths of upgrading in order that the better jobs may be given to the best qualified employees. Management must specify that those who operate this central service be consulted on all upgrading opportunities and that final action be approved by them. Any disagreement between the line organization and the central service moves up the line for review and final decision by top management. Such a plan can be set up quickly by assigning the responsibility to a man who has wide knowledge of jobs and workers in the plant. Increased experience with upgrading constantly raises the level of results.

SEE THAT EMPLOYEES ARE INSTRUCTED ON THE JOB

Experienced employees, as well as "green" workers, should be given careful instruction when moved to new jobs. Correct work procedures should be taught from the start. Typical instruction procedures are outlined in other Training Within Industry bulletins.

MAKE PRACTICAL USE OF SUPPLEMENTARY INSTRUCTION

Appropriate encouragement should be given to employees to pursue outside studies in preparation for greater usefulness. Local schools and colleges offer a wide variety of courses. Special courses can readily be organized in the plant, to be taught by foremen, engineers, inspectors, or others. Some unions also conduct such courses. Completion of supplementary courses should be shown on personnel records. (See Training Within Industry Bulletin, "Supplementary Training for Upgrading.")

MAKE PROMPT ADJUSTMENTS IN PAY

Pay adjustments should be made simultaneously with promotion to the jobs of higher rating. Prompt recognition in compensation and status are the means for stimulating and maintaining interest in the learning process. Morale will be high under this policy of advancement, based on the fair and unprejudiced consideration of merit. Where merit and other factors are equal, preference should be given to length of service. Periodic review of rates by the appropriate supervisor is essential to see that deserving employees aren't "forgotten" and that equity and fairness are maintained.

Such a policy of upgrading, coordinated by a central placement service, results in rapid and efficient training of a working force with greater flexibility and effectiveness. This is an important practice.

SUPPLEMENTARY INSTRUCTION FOR UPGRADING

21

America at war demands that every man and woman work at his or her top skill. Maximum production depends on maximum use of skill. The upgrading of workers to more skilled jobs requires the full cooperation of both employees and management. Management must be constantly on the job of discovering skills and placing and training its employees until everyone is doing the best job of which he is potentially capable. Similarly, the employee must avail himself of every opportunity to learn, on or off the job, both the technical skills and the supplementary knowledge necessary for advancement to the higher and more responsible jobs in his plant.

Training in the essential skills of a job is best done on the job, but the supplementary information which is a tool for a more demanding job is most often acquired off the job. Supplementary instruction is applicable at all levels of the organization and a necessary requirement for moving from one stage to that above. Time is wasted and lost, and so are skills, unless management encourages employees to help themselves through off–the–job instruction and integrates it with progression on the job.

The best interest of the worker, the best production by industry, the best service to our country depend largely on the BEST USE OF THE SKILLS of all our people.

C. R. Dooley, Director
Training Within Industry

RESPONSIBILITY FOR SUPPLEMENTARY INSTRUCTION

Every earnest worker expects to be promoted to a better job with better wages, as soon as he demonstrates that he can do that more responsible job and there is opportunity. The individual worker generally knows what his actual skills are and in what potential direction they lead. Therefore, much of the responsibility for supplementary instruction to develop his potential skill rests upon the employee himself.

While some employers provide both facilities and time for related instruction concerned with the job on which the employee is now working, the increasing necessity for maximum production means that this type of instruction will more and more be done after hours. And instruction which applies to the more advanced job will tend to be left even more to the ambition and initiative of the employee.

However, management can and should stimulate the employee to seek supplementary instruction outside the plant by:

1. Establishing and announcing the requirements for advanced jobs toward which the worker may strive

2. Publicizing the use management makes of information about out–of–hours instruction

3. Providing information about local opportunities for supplementary instruction

4. Giving financial assistance for or other recognition of outside study

Management can perform a useful function in coordinating such instruction by:

1. Guidance of outside study to tie in supplementary instruction with training received on the job

2. Making information about the employee's off–the–job instruction a part of the plant personnel records used when candidates for better jobs are considered.

THE REQUIREMENTS FOR ADVANCED JOBS

Each war industry has a vital and definite training job. Maximum results must be accomplished in record time. Upgrading is constantly necessary if war industry is to get results. An invaluable aid in securing the cooperation of employees in upgrading is the use of specifications giving essential requirements for jobs. Job specifications, listing the most important types of things each skilled worker does, should therefore be widely circulated among all employees. The worker then will know what information, skills, and aptitudes are required of him in order to secure an advanced job and will see what he has to do in order to fill that job.

Job specifications are also necessary for schools that offer supplementary instruction to workers. Properly prepared specifications furnish an accurate picture of specific skills required and may be used to outline a school program of progressing steps to develop the required skills and information quickly in wisely selected workers.

During the last war the Army wrote such specifications for the various jobs in military units. Schools used them, and extraordinary results were obtained. Skilled workers were trained in much less time than had ever been done before and more effectively than had ever been considered possible—in many instances the instruction period in schools was cut in half. Industry now recognizes its own need for job specifications but does not always make them available to employees or to schools.

We need to use specifications now as a medium of stimulation, inspiration, and incentive for the employee—in other words, we need them now, as a necessary tool in securing the worker's cooperation in his own upgrading. He needs to know just what the requirements are for successful performance right on the job.

In order to use supplementary instruction in the upgrading procedure, it is essential to study the progression that can be made if "something else" is added. The company training director should be responsible not only for collecting information about available supplementary instruction but he should present it to employees in a way which shows its relation to the factory jobs.

"Going to night school" is a good American custom—it will help America now if the young factory operator, for example, studies shop arithmetic or blueprint reading, and the ambitious supervisor adds to his knowledge of technical and personnel subjects.

INFORMATION ABOUT OUTSIDE INSTRUCTION

In helping employees (men and women) to plan their own off-the-job instruction intelligently, management through its training director or similar official will need an evaluation of instruction offered by outside agencies—public school evening courses, defense courses, government-sponsored adult education programs, programs of such groups as the Y.M.C.A., college extension programs, and so on. The district offices of the Training Within Industry Service furnish information on the amount, caliber, and cost of supplementary instruction.

COORDINATION OF SUPPLEMENTARY INSTRUCTION

Once the employee undertakes supplementary instruction in order to qualify for more skilled tasks, management must help to coordinate the employee's out–of–hours study in such manner that the supplementary work assists in the upgrading of the employee in minimum time.

Training is a management responsibility, When part of the employee's instruction comes from an outside source it is good business for the management to help in shaping the direction of off–the–job instruction. Well–written job specifications will help management to know what specific jobs require in special or technical knowledge. From this knowledge management can help the aspirant for any particular job to plan his supplementary instruction intelligently.

RECOGNIZING SUPPLEMENTARY INSTRUCTION IN PLANT RECORDS

The fact that a young operator, since his employment, has successfully studied blueprint reading and drafting is as necessary a part of the plant personnel records as the fact that before he was employed he was graduated from a high school. This off–the–job instruction has added to his ability and it has also given an indication of personal characteristics. Such instruction is therefore a very important part of the employee's personnel record. It is immediately useful to management for upgrading the employee. It is a powerful factor in morale-building because the employee knows that management recognizes that he is trying to improve himself not only on his present job but for the advanced job which he hopes to get.

The plant training man cannot pick up this information completely by any casual method. There must be a regular process or channel through which this information becomes part of the personnel records. This is valuable information for the company, and it is a builder of good will. Even if there has been no insurance, through a regular process of recording information on off–the–job instruction, that the company knows that a man has acquired a better background and that he has marked interest in his job, the man who is not considered for a job for which he knows he is qualified will feel resentment.

The company **can** guide its employees toward useful off–the–job study and it needs to set up a regular process to get information about the instruction which its employees are getting on their own. It must be made clear however, that this kind of related instruction is no guarantee for selection for the next vacancy; too many other factors are involved.

ASSISTANCE WITH THE EXPENSE OF OFF-THE-JOB INSTRUCTION

When a public agency supplies instruction which is useful to production, part of the load on plant management has been relieved. A number of companies feel it is a good investment to pay all or part of the fees which the employee must pay for supplementary instruction when such instruction follows an approved plan and is successfully completed.

PLANNING INTEGRATION OF SUPPLEMENTARY INSTRUCTION

With the increasing training load, it is necessary to assume that in each plant there is one person who has the responsibility for training (of course, in small plants, this may not be a full-time job). But one person cannot do the whole job of integrating supplementary instruction with production. Supervisors are in the best position to be helpful to those whose work they know.

Supervisors write job specifications or assist with them, and they will help most on job performance. If there is a joint training committee, it should be used to get employees' ideas on what they believe they need.

SUPPLEMENTARY INSTRUCTION'S IMPORTANCE TO A PLANT PROGRAM

Off-the-job instruction will do part of the training, and plant management needs to know what is available so that employees can be helped. But making information available does not insure that it gets across. Supplementary instruction must be *promoted*.

When supplementary instruction is planned, when it is integrated with the plant program, when it is *used*, it becomes an important part of the industrial training program.

Training on the job and supplementary instruction, when planned and tied in and used with the individual worker's best talents in view, result in real education for the individual—he is then at his best; he grows strong, works hard, and likes it.

TRAINING AIDS

22

While the bulk of the defense training must be done on the job by using actual machines and material, there are aids to this training which can be used to help a workman make rapid progress in acquiring skill and knowledge.

Some related scientific information, technical knowledge or a specific understanding of principles which a fully competent worker must possess, cannot be demonstrated very well while doing the actual work. Any suitable method which provides an understanding of such knowledge to those being trained will pay dividends in getting effective workers in a shorter time.

They are usually used in a suitable class or school–room under the leadership of an instructor, or at home by the learner himself.

C. R. Dooley, Director
Training Within Industry

There are several commonly accepted aids which have a recognized value in helping to train production specialists, all–round skilled workers, and supervisors. A typical group of these which have demonstrated their effectiveness are:

1) Standard Texts, Illustrations, Charts.
2) Libraries of reference books.
3) Prepared outlines and guides for conferences and meetings.
4) Motion pictures and slide films.

While not all of them may be found necessary in each training situation, it is frequently found that one or the other can contribute to a more complete understanding of the objective toward which the training is aimed.

STANDARD TEXTS

The use of such aids as handbooks, mathematical texts, treatments of metals or other materials, chemical and metallurgical processes, etc., are recognized as an aid in training and specific applications for them can readily be found in many training programs. These standard texts are used to supplement the training actually given in manipulative skill.

In some instances illustrations on a large scale specifically worked out to show the effects of certain operations, the structure and internal arrangement of machinery, as well as the places on machinery where lubrication or special care is necessary, all lend themselves to a use in supplementary training. In like manner, wall charts, or smaller sized charts, particularly referring to sizes of drills, taps and other tools, shop organization, production flow and a variety of other display matter may be effectively used.

LIBRARIES

Many industrial training programs have as part of their setup shop libraries in which selected books covering some of the related subjects are available for any employees use during out–of–work hours. In addition to these shop libraries, there is usually available in every locality public libraries which have books available on industrial subjects which cover a wide range of subject matter. Lists of these books are often prepared on a catalog basis which makes the selection of a particular volume easy to make.

In addition to the recognized standard text books, such libraries include pamphlets, periodicals, trade catalogs, shop manuals, and cuts and diagrams which are more current in their application than the more comprehensive standard texts.

Thus through books, charts and pictures, oftentimes the best possible technical information from schools, colleges and libraries is made available for men and women who are fitting themselves to work in defense industries.

CONFERENCE OUTLINES

In order to save time in setting up a complete training program, firms which do not have a very extensive background in training may obtain outlines which are available and which cover most of the usual training activities. In connection with supervisory training, a good deal of experience has been crystallized and is available in outline form. Lists of suggestive subject matter for discussion, arrangements of the order in which discussions may be best handled, together with guides for a conference leader, can also be secured. In like manner, outlines of training courses which have been developed and used by industrial firms have been prepared and can often be had by a firm in a similar line of production on direct application to these firms. Such material is also available from the state vocational departments and extension departments of some universities.

Such outlines should be viewed as guides for they rarely can be followed exactly as presented. They do, however, offer ground work aid in the setting up and conducting of a program to meet specific training needs.

MOTION PICTURES

For many subjects, particularly relating to scientific and technical information, the moving picture offers an excellent medium for presenting accurate information. Some work processes are also available, particularly metal work such as riveting, machine tool operations, punch press and assembly work.

There are a number of commercial producers of motion pictures who have lists of such subjects which can be considered if motion pictures seem to be suitable for best presenting a particular part of the information. The motion pictures may be accompanied by sound and often are made in natural colors. In addition to motion pictures, slide films, which, of course, show a series of still pictures usually accompanied by a lecture (recorded on discs), are also available covering a wide range of subjects.

Slide films and motion pictures, both silent and with sound effects, are available for presenting fundamentals of supervisory work on which much information is available through commercial producers.

The degree to which either or all of these aids can be used to advantage in training has to be decided by the particular firm considering it. In no case can such aids to training be considered as a substitute which will completely eliminate the need for specific instruction in the actual handling of tools and materials by an experienced operator or instructor.

HOW TO GET A PLANT TRAINING PLAN INTO ACTION

23

More training plans fail because they are poorly presented and inadequately sold to management than for any other reason. Each instance of this kind is unfortunate. Even more unfortunate are the good plans that operate half–heartedly, all for the lack of proper management support. This bulletin deals specifically with the problem of getting a training plan into action so it produces results.

When the training man does something *for* the line organization, the problem of selling is usually not too difficult. In such cases management often needs only to give approval. An example is approving a program of class instruction in any technical subject, like arithmetic or blueprint reading or electricity, or approving the use of engineering school extension facilities.

Those activities that a training man does *through* the line organization not only must be approved by management but must be done by management because they are a part of the management process.

C. R. Dooley, Director
Training Within Industry

STEPS IN GETTING A PLAN IN ACTION

The steps required to launch a training plan will vary according to the plan. The following outline covers the four basic steps which the training man commonly follows in order to get a plan into action:

1. Get top management support

2. Sell and inform middle management

3. Select and train the instructors or conference leaders

4. Schedule sessions

This material will be useful to training men in large or small companies—whether they have full or part-time responsibility—whether or not they are called training men—in fact to anyone responsible for training in a staff capacity, who wants to get results *through* the line organization.

GETTING TOP MANAGEMENT SUPPORT

Top management is the operating official who has the final authority to say "yes" or "no" on any question that requires management approval.

WHAT PREPARATION SHOULD BE MADE PRIOR TO THE INTERVIEW?

This is often the key to the success of the whole program. Be clear in your own mind just what is to be accomplished. In practically every case there are just two end objectives: to secure acceptance of the training plan, and to secure agreement to sponsor it.

Before arranging to present a plan to management, the training man must plan how he will carry out the following steps:

1. Outline a plan and the mechanics of the necessary procedures for keeping the plan in action.

2. Establish the duties of persons with *staff* responsibility for keeping the plan in continuing operation.

3. Establish the duties of those with *line* or operating responsibility for keeping the plan in continuing operation.

4. Outline a plan to evaluate the results in terms of measurable data:

production increases   savings in machine use

reduction in "break–in"   time fewer accidents

savings in scrap   less fatigue

savings in manpower   reduction of grievances

5. Get management agreement to review these results at regular periods as a basis of giving encouragement and backing.

6. Establish procedure for getting reports of results and production benefits routed to the top executive.

Supporting material and exhibits must be ready. The value of such materials varies according to the man using them and also according to the executive to be sold. Some supporting materials which might be used are:

results reports from other industries
charts of production problems and their solution through training
samples of the materials to be used in the training plan

HOW SHOULD THE INTERVIEW BE CONDUCTED?

Each interview differs according to the personal relationships existing. The following points cover many of the important details:

1. **STATE PURPOSE OF THE MEETING:** Some executives want to get the recommendation or proposition stated in a point–blank manner at the beginning. Others want background before hearing your plan or conclusions.

2. **BUILD THE ADVANTAGES TO HIM AND TO THE ORGANIZATION:** Sell him on what the training will do: Talk about the **problem** you have to discuss—not "Training." Avoid arguments—use the "yes–but" approach.

3. **GET A DECISION:**

   a) Tell him how it works—outline the mechanics you recommend, i.e., your recommendation for leaders, sessions, and the like.

   b) Secure his definite acceptance—ask him to approve or designate the individuals who will assist in the plan.

   c) Establish his responsibility for getting the plan off to a good start. Get him to agree to: personally sponsor the plan, approve the details, and call and chairman the meeting at which it will be launched (set definite date if possible).

   d) Establish his responsibility for getting CONTINUING results.

Beware of too ready acceptance—of too ready a "yes." Many a training man has been swept off his feet by a top executive who agreed to everything promptly, or said or implied, "You just go right ahead and do it." Then back in his own office the training man realized that, instead of getting the boss to take the lead, he was to take the lead.

Perhaps the executive will not give final agreement until the matter is discussed with the executive staff. If this is the case, arrange for such a meeting immediately. Cover the complete story with the executive group.

SELLING AND INFORMING MIDDLE MANAGEMENT

A meeting with executives is conducted to get group approval of the training plan, to convince them of its value, and to secure the maximum possible understanding and cooperation of all management. It is necessary for a specific date and time to be set and a satisfactory meeting room arranged. The meeting must be called by the *top executive* over *his signature.*

WHAT SHOULD BE COVERED IN SUCH A MEETING?

The introduction should be made by the sponsoring executive. The plan is presented by the training man, the industrial relations director, the works manager, or by the person who carries the most weight and who can be persuaded to do the job. This presentation should cover (1) what the training will do in terms of production benefits, (2) what it is, and (3) what must be done by management to make the plan function as a continuing production tool.

SELECTING AND TRAINING LEADERS

WHO SHOULD SELECT THE PROSPECTIVE INSTRUCTORS OR LEADERS?

The use of special leaders or instructors is not a required part of every program, of course. The initial list should be put together by the training man. Depending on the size of the plant, he should get the counsel of others regarding the ability of each proposed leader. The final act of selecting and notification should be done by each prospective leader's own boss.

WHO MAKE THE BEST LEADERS?

Personal characteristics are among the most important considerations:

1. Operating men often make excellent leaders. However, some operating people are too busy and are victims of too many pressures.

2. "Acceptability" of the leaders can be a controlling factor.

3. The all–round ability of a prospect is the most important consideration. The job must be done by those who "can't be spared." The program fails if done by those "who haven't much to do any how."

4. Competent staff people often can give time more readily and can do the best leadership job.

DO LEADERS NEED ANY SPECIAL PREPARATION?

Even if the meetings are not more than staff meetings with their own people, leaders need some help. If they are to hold special meetings or if they are to become trainers for any of the T.W.I. programs, they need even more attention. The training man must arrange for the special coaching to be given to the leaders. This coaching may vary from a short one–hour explanation of the company's plan for handling returning veterans, to a five or six–day Institute on how to successfully conduct one of the 10–hour T.W.I. programs.

Prior to the beginning of their preparation to handle a new program, the prospective leaders should be called together and all points connected with "who does what, and when" cleared up. At this meeting, the training man can "size up" the group and perhaps pick out those who won't make the grade. It will save time and embarrassment to him and the prospective leaders if this can be tactfully handled ahead of time.

GETTING SESSIONS PROPERLY SCHEDULED

WHEN SHOULD SESSIONS BE SCHEDULED?

BEFORE the prospective leader or trainer attends the special leaders' conference, all arrangements for sessions he will put on MUST be completed. The leader loses his enthusiasm if he has to wait a week or two before he puts on his first session. As a result, he has forgotten many of the fine points; his mind becomes occupied with other things, and he does a mediocre job.

WHAT MUST BE CONSIDERED IN SCHEDULING SESSIONS?

1) Number of supervisors or others to be trained.

2) Timetable for coverage, starting dates, and starting groups.

3) Determination as to whether training is to be during working hours or out of hours—management should be urged to compensate supervisors for any out–of–hours time spent on basic training.

4) Selection of meeting rooms and checking of equipment.

5) Notification of persons who are to meet in each group (such notification should come from each person's boss).

SUMMARY

Any training program that involves supervisory practice throughout the plant is a big job. One of the difficulties with the training function in most companies is that training men and management alike take a superficial view. Influencing the way men conduct their daily jobs is, in actual fact, one of the most difficult undertakings in the whole field of industrial management. Any training man who wants to measure up to the size of the job that he holds should start by recognizing with great confidence yet humility that the job is big and is difficult, and that he can only hope to get it done through the line organization. An "expert on training" cannot do it all himself.

HOW TO GET CONTINUING RESULTS FROM PLANT TRAINING PROGRAMS

24

Plans for using the knowledge and skill acquired through training must be approved at the same time as plans for training are adopted. There are four fundamental things that the *LINE* organization must do to assure that results are obtained:

1. Assign responsibility.

2. Get adequate coverage.

3. Provide for coaching.

4. Report results and give credit.

"Continuing results" are obtained in various ways. A company may take various means to see that the supervisors and the workers who have been instructed—either in group sessions or through personal instruction—*use* what they have learned. Naturally the only persons who can *insist on use and build real values* are those in the *LINE* organization.

However, a *staff* person usually has an important place in helping the plant to get results. Such a staff person gets his management to remind the line organization from time to time that continuing results are expected. The staff person should never do this reminding. He also provides technical assistance to the line organization on exactly *HOW* to use the training that has been received.

The way of providing this continuing attention and assistance varies from plant to plant. One manager, for example, may keep company activities going mainly by means of reports and will want to emphasize reports on results training. Another manager does this by means of periodic meetings—each according to his habit in handling other production matters.

C. R. Dooley, Director
Training Within Industry Service

FUNDAMENTALS FOR GETTING CONTINUING RESULTS

There are four fundamental points that must be carried out in order to get continuing results from any training:

1. ASSIGN RESPONSIBILITY FOR GETTING CONTINUING RESULTS

The sponsoring executive must make it clear to the members of the executive and supervisory staff that they are responsible for results. Many top executives call a meeting of all those in the middle management group for this purpose.

To get the top executive to take appropriate action on this fundamental, the training director can get a decision by discussing the present procedure for informing the executive and supervisory organization of *any* new responsibility or a new policy.

2. GET ADEQUATE COVERAGE

In any training program, adequate coverage means training for every person who needs the specific knowledge or skill *and* for their superiors to the extent needed by them in order that they support the program. In addition to getting adequate coverage in the training sessions, refresher or "brush up" sessions are often used to advantage.

Getting adequate coverage is often necessary before it becomes possible to do much in the way of assuring continuing results. It should be made clear that the more every supervisor and every executive knows about the particular training program, the better he can supervise its application for continuing results.

Many programs fail to get results because the coverage was not adequate, and there was not sufficient participation far enough up the line. Top executives take interest in scrap, accident rates, etc., should they have less information about the steps taken to overcome these problems?

3. PROVIDE FOR COACHING

Supervisors generally provide assistance to their subordinates on *all* day-to-day operating matters. Similar assistance should be provided on those phases of the operating job that have been emphasized and "sharpened up" through specific training. Coaching, therefore, should be given to supervisors and workers by their own bosses. This is the procedure to be recommended and "sold" whenever possible because it gets the best results. Coaching includes not only the refinement of the content material, but the development of desire and interest in the value of the training to the individual.

Every supervisor (the same as every worker) reflects the thinking of his boss. If *his boss* shows interest, *he* shows interest. If *his boss* considers a matter important, *he* likely considers it important. Coaching by the boss demonstrates that the company really "means business."

The training director usually assists the line organization by providing a simple, specific coaching procedure—one that will clarify any misunderstandings and re-emphasize all basic points—but line executives themselves should do the coaching. Details on coaching are given in the next section of this bulletin.

4. REPORT RESULTS TO MANAGEMENT AND GIVE CREDIT

Appropriate executives should be informed as to results of any training in order to give suitable support. Busy executives need to know what is going on so they can appraise results. Experience has shown that wherever continuing results are obtained there is a flow of definite information to executives about these results.

When discussing with a plant executive results to be expected, it must be remembered that many influences in a plant may contribute to certain results. Training programs help get better results, of course, but should never be presented as the only means for complete solution of all production problems.

Prompt and proper recognition by the appropriate executive is necessary to obtain continuing interest and, hence, continuing results.

Again, how often and by what means credit is to be given are decisions each company must make. The giving of credit is perhaps the most powerful force that can operate to stimulate interest, enthusiasm, and continued action.

PROVISION FOR COACHING

Coaching is the third of the fundamentals for getting continuing results mentioned on the previous page. There are two objectives in any coaching procedure.

> To give the supervisor a renewed understanding of how to improve his use of what he has learned in the training program, and to stimulate interest and desire to use the training based on the results to him personally.

Whether this understanding is gotten over to each person individually or is given to several in a small group is a matter to be decided in each instance. The one essential is to get a thorough understanding of the program and its value.

HOW TO COACH

Getting a negligent worker or supervisor to promise to "do better" or "showing him how" is not coaching. The objective of any coaching is to have each person understand and use what he has learned.

As an example, it has been found that, in increasing the skills of instruction, of improving methods, and of leading, the following five coaching steps are adequate and effective. It is not expected that all five items will be used in the order listed or that all five will be covered at any one contact. Naturally, the coach must be thoroughly grounded in the particular program before he can use the coaching technique.

1. GIVE REASONS AND ADVANTAGES WHY PROGRAM SHOULD BE USED

Good tangible reasons for using the program under discussion, based on specific departmental experience if possible, should be presented—typical reasons such as:

Less tool breakage	Better use of manpower	Fewer misfits
Fewer accidents	Savings in materials	Fewer gripes
Less scrap	Better use of space	Fewer grievances
Shorter break-in time	Less turnover	More production per machine–hour

2. GET UNDERSTANDING OF THE PRINCIPLES

It is essential to review the basic principles or chief points of the program. Every point should be clarified. A good way to determine whether the program is understood is to ask questions about various points. The application of the various points to some current problem or situation makes them practical and vital. Always use plenty of "reasons why."

3. SELECT A PROBLEM AND WORK ON IT TOGETHER

This is the most helpful coaching device that can be provided. The person may need help in identifying a problem. Whatever the problem that is identified, nothing shows so clearly the usefulness of the training program as working it out together. Working it out together should mean that the coach offers guidance and assistance but does *NOT* do much of the work himself. The coach sees that the METHOD is used; the supervisor makes the application.

4. ASK HIM TO WORK OUT ANOTHER PROBLEM ALONE

Another problem should be identified and the person being coached is asked to go ahead and work it out alone. This will increase his confidence in his own ability. It also provides a logical reason for agreeing to check with each other at a later date.

5. GIVE HIM CREDIT FOR GOOD RESULTS AND GOOD EFFORT

Appropriate credit should be given according to plant custom. Often a determined effort to apply a program in the face of many difficulties is as worthy of credit as actual results. The giving of credit should not, of course, be overdone. The thought should be left that these occasional checks are never to be concluded. The supervisor being coached should understand that he is expected to use what he has learned in the program, that he will be checked as to his use of it, and that he can receive some tips on *HOW* to use it, month after month, presumably as long as the supervisory relationship is maintained.

HOW TO MEET SPECIFIC NEEDS

25

You are faced with meeting a definite responsibility your management has assigned. Training is an everyday part of getting out the work. A training program is simply *managements organized attention* to the problems related to introduction, instruction, and coaching the individual workers and supervisors.

Every supervisor has a part if the training program is well set up and coordinated. Your job is to help each supervisor to meet his responsibility. You *can* help him by doing some things for him, but the biggest help is to *equip* each supervisor with *knowledge, tools,* and *skills* which will enable him to *make the most effective use of the manpower under his supervision.*

The business of your plant *is* different. Even though the finished product

147

is the same as in some other plant, there are many internal factors that control the effectiveness from a production point of view. These must be dealt with in your specific plans. Here are some ideas and methods of attack that have proven useful in many companies. They can be adapted to your program if you clearly understand the specific needs of your own plant which can be met through training.

C. R. Dooley, Director
Training Within Industry Service

WHAT TRAINING IS NEEDED IN YOUR PLANT?

Is your plant the same as it was in 1940? Or did you have a plant in 1940? If you are in an organization which has been in existence for some years, and you still work in the same building that you did before the war, are you making the same product? And do you have the same operators, craftsmen, and supervisors as you had two years ago? Or, were you a training director in the old days?

No war contractor in the country can say "yes" to all these questions. We all have new jobs, new equipment, new people. *We have a training job.*

IDENTIFYING TRAINING NEEDS

Each plant has training problems of its own. The product it manufactures, the materials and machinery used, the men and women who turn out the work—all these combine to make the situation in *your* plant different. The training director of the plant is the one management holds responsible for looking closely at just what his *own* plant needs.

PLANNING A PROGRAM

In order to meet the needs of your plant, you must first spot the *specific* needs—the ones which need your attention now. Training is planned by deciding on the content, who will be trained, who will do the training and when, how, and where it should be carried out. But there is no training done unless the training plan is sold to management and gets support not only from the top but down through the line organization. And, of course, all training must be checked for results.

No single training plan stands alone. You cannot start to train supervisors one day, and set up to produce skilled mechanics on the next, and arrange for a local vocational school to give related instruction without considering their effect on each other. And you cannot ignore the drain you put on supervision if you involve certain supervisors in too many parts of a program at once.

Your program must be coordinated to use the talent in the plant in ways which will help the line organization to get out production.

148

WHAT ARE "TRAINING NEEDS?"

The training director has to plan his own program—but he *can* check the common needs found in most plants. He then has a start on planning the way he will meet his *own* plant's needs. You get your best tips in terms of things that are interfering with production—turnover, accidents, rejected work, tool breakage, scrap, errors in following instructions, poor interdepartmental relations. These must be improved through organized training.

INDUCTION OF NEW WORKERS

Getting on to "the way of doing things" is one of the most important factors in getting the new worker off to a good start. Whether you plan it or not, every person whom the new employee meets when he first comes to your plant gives him some information or impression of the place where he is starting to work.

Are there things *you* want him to know? Are there rules *you* will expect him to live up to? Of course, there are. And do you suppose *he* wants to also know such things as just how he is supposed to conduct himself? Or when and where and how he gets his pay? What he should wear on the job? Whether there are any privileges or penalties about his new job?

Would you like him to get this information that he wants or needs from someone who will give it to him straight—or do you want to leave it for chance remarks, perhaps from some worker (who, though older in service, may not be too sure about the answers?)

An induction plan is just the simple giving of attention to the necessity of providing a definitely coordinated way for the new man or woman to learn what he needs to know, when he needs to know it.

TRAINING OF NON-SUPERVISORY EMPLOYEES

Information about the plant is not all that the new worker needs. He must learn to do a job which will contribute to the whole war production of the plant. Perhaps your plant used to have men who carried on a series of operations. When the new women come in, you may need to train each of them to do a single job.

You have to know what specific jobs are being filled by new people—and *you* have to know what it takes to do that job. Then too, these days, many of your experienced people are being transferred to jobs new to them. These are training needs easy to identify and to plan to meet.

Is every person in your plant working full time at his highest skill? Or does someone spend valuable time on jobs which could just as well be performed by a less-skilled person? Both good business and good relations require that we use people at their highest skills.

But using highest skills is not enough. Sometimes we have to "produce skills." Amazing production records can be achieved by engineering jobs so that relatively new people can be instructed quickly to perform individual operations. But the plant *still needs skilled craftsmen*. It would be shortsighted if we failed to build our supply of all–round skilled workers through well planned upgrading and apprentice programs.

Much plant time can be saved if the public training courses for pre–production and supplementary instruction are utilized. For example, on some jobs ability to read blueprints is necessary—and how to read a blueprint can be learned in a school before coming to work.

Many public training agencies are really doing *production* training where they set up shops which give the person new to industry familiarity with machines and operations. In order for a worker to be upgraded to a more difficult job he may need some training which he can get off the job. *Do you know the facilities* which are available in your community? Do the training agencies *know what you need?* And are your workers fully informed of how they can take advantage of these opportunities?

IMPROVING SUPERVISOR'S KNOWLEDGE OF WORK AND RESPONSIBILITIES

Supervisors are not usually thought of as skilled workers, but to do their jobs they certainly *need skills*. Skills are not enough. Some things they just have to *know*. They must know their own work—what goes on in their departments—what it *takes* to turn out production—just what men and women in their departments must be able to do. And they must know just what is *expected* of them as management's representatives. They have to know what they are responsible for, and only their own plant operating executives can tell them.

A big training field here is often ignored by assuming that "the supervisors know, or else they wouldn't be supervisors." It is *your job*, as training director, to provide a *way* for them to acquire what they need to know.

TRAINING SUPERVISORS TO CONDUCT MEETINGS

Do your supervisors ever have to get any information across to a group of people? Or do they ever try to get a department to accept some change? Or do you use supervisors to help on parts of various kinds of programs?

Skilled "conference leaders" are rare. They grow through experience. But some simple techniques are easy to acquire, and they are of value in any plant. Supervisors gain confidence through using them. If the people to whom you assign training responsibility cannot "put it across," your training program may fail.

IMPROVING INSTRUCTION ON THE JOB

Training Within Industry's program for Job Instruction is used in many war production plants. But is *your plant* getting full value out of this simple but effective way to break in a new man on a new job?

INCREASE THE SUPERVISOR'S SKILL OF IMPROVING METHODS

Job Methods Training may be new in your plant. Would it help to see that the *right* people get Job Methods Training? And that they *use* it? It will help them to avoid waste of machine time, materials and workers' efforts.

150

COACHING IN EVERYDAY RELATIONS ON THE JOB

Job Relations Training will help your supervisors to acquire skill in working with individuals and groups. Constant use of basic fundamentals of good relations will also prevent many problems.

SELECTING NEW SUPERVISORS

Do you ever have to appoint new supervisors in your plant? Almost every day, it seems. Yesterday they were operators—today they are in charge of units. Even if the plant has provided a way to train those beginning supervisors in the skills and knowledge that they need—is that *enough*? Are you *sure* that you are training the right people?

There is a simple means that the training director can use to spot among the rank–and–file workers those who are the best bets for the fulfilling of supervisory responsibility. Sponsoring and using such a plan is a definite part of a comprehensive training program.

ORGANIZING THE PLANT PROGRAM

When you have identified the training needed in your plant, and planned ways of training to meet those needs—you still must *organize* your plan into an overall program. There may be a man who is the very best in the plant to get a new person off to the right start, who is splendid in working with the public schools in planning related instruction, who really knows just what is expected of a supervisor in this particular plant. Are you going to use him for all those jobs? You probably cannot.

You may have hundreds of new employees coming into your plant every week. There is much about your own establishment to learn. Are you going to give it all to them at once? Probably not. You may need production operators, and job instructors, and set–up men, and supervisors. Where do you get started?

Organizing a plant training program is simply planning *Who* does *What*, and *When* and *Where*. What happens next depends on the understanding and backing the program gets from the entire executive and supervisory staff.

RESPONSIBILITY FOR RESULTS THROUGH TRAINING

The LINE organization has the responsibility for making continuing use of the knowledge and skills acquired through training as a regular part of the operating job.

A STAFF group (or often one staff person) provides plans and technical "know how"; does some things *for* but usually works *through* the line organization.

INDEX

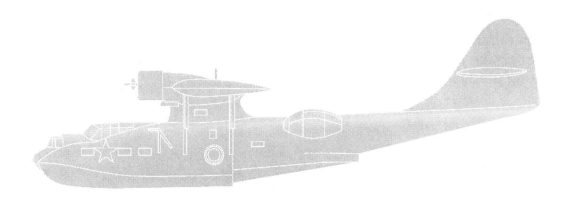

A

B

C

D

E

F

G

H

I

J

Q

Quality
  as elementary supervisory work 19
  meeting standards 17
  of supervision 3
  special cautions to ensure 40
  supervisors record of 46

R

Rearrange
  details for improved sequence 8, 34
Recognizing supplementary instruction in plant records 128
Respect 38, 46, 98
Responsibilities
  industrial training 14
  keeping Supervisors informed 59–62, 150
  operating 21

S

Safety 7, 8, 40, 68, 80, 92, 97, 106, 108–113
  and personnel records 47
Safety in hazardous plants 111
Selling and informing middle management 138
Simplify
  all necessary details 8, 34
  and improve job methods 2
Skills
  and pre-employment training 80
  acquired through training 11
  discovering 125
  learning by doing 55
  taking an inventory of 14
  workers who want to master 122
Skill in improving methods 4
Skill in instructing 4
Skill in working with people 4
Sound practices 22
Status and pay 23
Supervisor's Five Needs 3
Supervisory pool 50
Systemizing the introduction process 104

Publications from Enna

From Enna's new classics by Shigeo Shingo to our Lean Origin Series, Enna provides companies with the foundation of knowledge and practical implementation ideas that will ensure your efforts to internalize process improvement. Reach your vision and mission with the expertise within these world-class texts. Call toll-free (866) 249-7348 or visit us on the web at www.enna.com to order or request our free product catalog.

Books

Kaizen and the Art of Creative Thinking

Read the book that New York Times Best Selling author of *The Toyota Way*, Jeffrey Liker says, "will help you understand the deep thinking that underlies the real practice of TPS." Dr. Shigeo Shingo's Scientific Thinking Mechanism is the framework from which Toyota and hundreds of other companies have utilized to manage creative problem solving.

ISBN 978-1-897363-59-1 | 2007 | $59.40 | Item: **909**

Organizing for Work

When approached from the Lean perspective, H. L. Gantt's Organizing for Work provides a window into the American origins of the 2nd Pillar of Lean – Respect For People. Gantt, the creator of Gantt charts, galvanized the human aspect of efficiency with razor sharp clarity. Production improvements go astray because, we have "ignored the human factor and failed to take advantage of the ability and desire of the ordinary man to learn and improve his position."

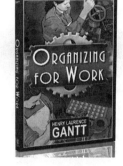

ISBN 978-1-897363-80-5 | 2007 | $59.40 | Item: **910**

The Principles of Scientific Management

Read the American classic that inspired Shigeo Shingo! Frederick W. Taylor's *The Principles of Scientific Management*, was a mental revolution that spawned the very ideas of process improvement, equity and efficiency between workers and management, and the attainability of high production with low labor costs. As the basis of modern organizational efficiency, this instrumental book has motivated managers and engineers for almost 100 years.

ISBN 978-1-897363-89-8 | 2008 | $21.99| Item: **912**

Tel: (866) 249-7348   Fax: (905) 481-0756   Web: info@enna.com

Shop Management

Shop Management is a manual that goes into the nuts and bolts of efficiency and improvement. Like every good consultant, he sums up big ideas with concise points and principles. Frederick W. Taylor's Four Principles of Organizational Change should be hung in any environment where improvements are sought:
1. Choose a specific management style
2. It takes money
3. It takes time
4. Consistent and respectful implementation

ISBN 978-1-897363-90-4 | 2008 | $21.99| Item: **907**

The Strategos Guide to Value Stream & Process Mapping

The Strategos Guide to Value Stream and Process Mapping has proven strategies and helpful tips on facilitating group VSM exercises and puts VSM in the greater Lean context. With photos and examples of related Lean practices, the book focuses on implementing VSM, not just drawing diagrams and graphs.

ISBN 978-1-897363-43-0 | 2007 | $47.00 | Item: **905**

The Idea Generator, Quick and Easy Kaizen

The book discusses the Kaizen mind set that enables a company to utilize its resources to the fullest by directly involving all of its manpower in the enhancement and improvement of the productivity of its operations. Published and co–written by Norman Bodek, the *Godfather of Lean*.

ISBN 978-0971243699 | 2001 | $47.52 | Item: **902**

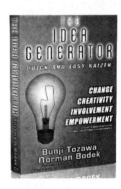

JIT is Flow

Hirano's *5 Pillars of the Visual Workplace* and *JIT Implementation Manual* were classics. They contained detailed descriptions of techniques and clear instructions. However, Hirano's books were difficult to adapt to many sectors. This book highlights the depth of the thought process behind Hirano's work. The know-how that is contained in this book is extremely useful. The clarity which Hirano brings to JIT/Lean and the delineation of the principles involved will be invaluable to every leader and manager aiming for business excellence.

ISBN 978-0971243613 | 2006 | $47.52 | Item: **903**

Training Materials

Jit Factory Flow Kit

If your company is serious about implementing a Lean Transformation, every person should go through this training. This hands–on simulation demonstrates the effectiveness of Just in Time manufacturing compared to normal manufacturing; it shows how much easier job functions can be and how efficient all employees can become if the simple and easy rules of JIT are followed. It is dynamic enough for high–level management training, yet has enough detail for production staff as well. We at Enna encourage all our customers to purchase this product as it provides the "Ah–ha, I get it!" factor for all your employees. In less than two hours you will have all your staff agreeing to move to a Lean Production System.

ISBN 978-1-897363-60-7 | 2007 | $479.99 | Item: **1081**

5S Training Package

Our 5S Solution Packages will help your company create a sustainable 5S program that will turn your shop floor around, and put you ahead of the competition. All of the benefits that come from Lean Manufacturing are built upon a strong foundation of 5S. The success or failure of all improvement initiatives can be traced to the robustness of 5S programs. Enna's solution packages will show you how to implement and sustain an environment of continuous improvement.

Version 1: ISBN 978-0-973750-90-4 | 2005 | $429.99 | Item: **12**
Version 2: ISBN 978-1-897363-25-6 | 2006 | $429.99 | Item: **17**

Version 1: Sort, Straighten, Sweep, Standardize, and Sustain
Version 2: Sort, Set In Order, Shine, Standardize, and Sustain

To Order:

Phone, fax, email, or mail to Enna Products Corporation ATTN: Order Processing, 1602 Carolina Street, Unit B3, Bellingham, WA, 98229 USA. Phone: (866) 249-7348, Fax: (905) 481-0756, Email: info@enna.com. Send checks to this address. We accept all major credit cards.

Notice:

All prices are in US dollars and are subject to change without notice.

CPSIA information can be obtained at www.ICGtesting.com
260336BV00002B/1-74/P

9 781897 363911